Alarms and Excursions

More plays than one

Michael Frayn

Samuel French — London
New York - Toronto - Hollywood

ALARMS AND EXCURSIONS

First presented at the Yvonne Arnaud Theatre in Guildford, on 15th July 1998 with the following cast:

Actor A	Nicky Henson
Actress B	Felicity Kendal
Actor C	Robert Bathurst
Actress D	Josie Lawrence

Directed by Michael Blakemore
Designed by Lez Brotherston
Lighting by Paul Pyant

Subsequently presented at the Gielgud Theatre, London, on 14th September 1998, with the same cast.

COPYRIGHT INFORMATION

(See also page ii)

CHARACTERS

ACT I

ALARMS

Nicholas
John
Jocasta
Nancy

DOUBLES

Miles
Melanie
Laurence
Lynn

ACT II

LEAVINGS

Nicholas
Nancy
Jocasta
John

LOOK AWAY NOW

Aptly
Bloss
Charr
Voice of Stewardess

HEART TO HEART

Clifford
Charmian
Peter

GLASSNOST

The Right Honourable the Baroness Armament KO
GBH RSVP

TOASTERS

Spott
Much
Candle
Voice of Speaker

IMMOBILES

Dietrich
Chris
Nikki
Mother

The plays are to be performed by a team of two actors and two actresses: **Actor A** and **Actress B**, both in their mid-forties; **Actor C** and **Actress D**, both in their mid-thirties.

The likely distribution of parts would be:

ACT I

	Actor A	Actress B	Actor C	Actress D
Alarms	John	Jocasta	Nicholas	Nancy
Doubles	Laurence	Lynn	Miles	Melanie

ACT II

	Actor A	Actress B	Actor C	Actress D
Leavings	John	Jocasta	Nicholas	Nancy
Look Away Now	Aptly	Charr	Bloss	Stewardess
Heart to Heart	Peter	—	Clifford	Charmian
Glassnost	Voice over PA	Lady Armament	—	—
Toasters	Speaker	Spott	Much	Candle
Immobiles	Chris	Mother	Dietrich	Nikki

The action takes place in a dining-room (**Alarms** and **Leavings**), two hotel bedrooms (**Doubles**), a commercial aircraft (**Look Away Now**), a reception room (**Heart to Heart**), on a stage (**Glassnost**), in a room at a business conference (**Toasters**) and in the environs of twelve different telephones (**Immobiles**).

Time — the present

Other plays by Michael Frayn
published by Samuel French Ltd

Alphabetical Order
Benefactors
Clouds
Donkeys Years
Make and Break
Noises Off
Now You Know
Number One (*translated from the Jean Anouilh original*)

ACT I

ALARMS

A dining-room. Evening

There are three entrances: R, L *and* C. *There is a dining-table with four chairs. On the table are a bottle of wine and an ingenious new corkscrew. There is a phone and answering machine*

When the play begins, the stage is empty

From off L *comes the sound of the front door opening and guests arriving*

Jocasta enters R

Nicholas and Nancy enter L, *ushered in by John*

Nicholas Just us?
John Just you.
Jocasta Is that all right?
Nancy Wonderful.
Nicholas Perfect.
John We thought we'd simply flop down exhausted in our braces.
Jocasta Have a nice quiet evening together.
John Four old chums, four weary fellow-travellers on the road of life, taking shelter for an hour or two from the night and storm.
Jocasta Something very simple in the oven.
Nancy Smells heavenly.
John The odd bottle of wine. (*He fetches the bottle*)
Nicholas More and more like heaven.
Jocasta Just have a look at the oven ...

Jocasta exits R

John Just open the wine ... (*He fetches the corkscrew, and sets to work with it during the following*) Then we can all ...
Nicholas Flop down.
Nancy Exhausted.

John In our braces.
Nicholas Where?
John What?
Nicholas Where do you want us to flop down?
John Anywhere. On the floor. Under the sideboard. On a chair ... On a chair!
Why not?
Nicholas On a chair!
Nancy Brilliant.
Nicholas Any chair?
John Absolutely any chair that takes your fancy.
Nicholas The man's a prince.

Jocasta enters R

Jocasta You found somewhere to park?
Nicholas Right outside.
Nancy For once!
John An augury, perhaps.
Nicholas This is going to be one of the great evenings.
John I'll just get the wine open ... (*He struggles with the corkscrew*) Then
we'll simply sit and ... I don't know ...

A sound. Chink

Jocasta Whatever one does when one gets the chance at last.
Nancy What *does* one do, as a matter of fact?
Nicholas So long since it happened.

Chink

Jocasta Talk, perhaps?
Nancy Talk, yes! Talk, talk, talk!
Jocasta I remember talk.
Nicholas Get the wine open, possibly.
John Get the wine open, certainly. (*He renews his efforts with the corkscrew*)
Nicholas Or not even talk. Sit here in silence, why not?

Chink

Nancy Relax. Be.
Nicholas Sip our wine.

John withdraws his fingers sharply from the corkscrew

Nicholas New toy?
John The point is you don't have to do all that heaving and cursing. You just
     quite simply ... No, hold on ... Or possibly ...
Nicholas Don't you put the ... And then ...?
John I've got it, I've got it ...
Nicholas No.
John Or ...
Nicholas Try ...
John Where are the instructions?
Jocasta I put them in the drawer.
John In the drawer?
Jocasta With all the other instructions.

Jocasta exits

Nicholas Give it to me.
John It's all right.
Nicholas Let me have a go!
John No, if I can just ...

Chink

   What?
Nicholas What?
John You made a little noise.
Nicholas No?
John It wasn't you?
Nicholas What sort of noise?
John Sort of — chink.

Chink

   There!
Nicholas I thought that was you.
John Me? Going chink?

Jocasta enters, with the instructions

Jocasta The instructions for everything — in the drawer.
Nicholas Did you hear it?
Jocasta Did I hear what?
John Chink.
Jocasta Chink?

Nancy Chink.
Jocasta What do you mean, chink?

Chink

Nancy There!
Jocasta What is it?
John That's what we want to know.
Nicholas Something in the house.
Nancy Some electronic thing.
Nicholas The phone.
John The phone? Phones don't go ——

Chink

Nicholas Listen!
John I've never heard a phone go chink!
Nancy But you've got this special system.
Nicholas This wonderful system.
Nancy That sends calls all over the house.
John Yes, but it doesn't go ——

Chink

It *is* you!
Nicholas It is *not* me!
John Something in your pocket.
Jocasta A pager, maybe.
Nicholas I haven't got a pager.
Nancy You've got your ——
Nicholas What?
Nancy — little whatsit thing.
Nicholas What — this?
Nancy No ...
Nicholas This?
John Pocketsful of the stuff.
Nancy That's electronic.
Nicholas Yes, but it doesn't go ——

Chink

Nancy What — me?
Jocasta Something in your bag.

Nancy Don't be silly.
Nicholas Let's have a look.
Nancy No!
Nicholas *I* got everything out of *my* pockets.
Nancy I don't keep things like that in my bag! There's nothing in there that
  could possibly go ——

Chink

Nicholas It's the opening thing.
John The opening thing?
Nicholas Your new bottle-opening thing.
John Going chink?
Nicholas To remind you.
John To do what?
Nicholas To open the wine.
Jocasta Yes. Come on.

Chink, chink

Nicholas There! Twice! Chink chink! It's getting desperate!
Jocasta No, but as soon as you touched it!
Nancy Try not touching it!
Nicholas Put it down!
Nancy Listen ... !
Nicholas Silence.
Nancy Wait ... Wait ...
Nicholas You see?
Nancy If you don't touch it it doesn't go ——

Chink

Nicholas It's the oven.
Jocasta The oven?
Nancy You said you've got something in the oven.
Jocasta The oven doesn't go ——

Chink

Nancy No, but the timer thing.
Jocasta The timer thing? The timer thing goes ——

There is a buzz (continuous)

Jocasta Excuse me ...

Jocasta exits R

Nancy *Something* in the kitchen, though. The microwave.
Nicholas Or the food-processor.
Nancy The coffee-maker.
Nicholas The coffee-grinder.

The buzzing stops

Nancy The toaster.
Nicholas The toaster?
John How can a toaster go —— ?

Chink

Jocasta enters R

Jocasta Anyway, let's all just forget about it.
John But it's plainly trying to tell us something.
Jocasta But if we don't know what it is ...
Nicholas It could be something important.
Jocasta It can't be *that* important!
John But it's plainly *meaningful*!

Silence

Nancy Listen!
Nicholas What?
Nancy It's stopped.

Silence

Jocasta Right. It's stopped. Where were we? What were we talking about?
Nancy The chink.
Jocasta Before that.
Nicholas I can't remember.
Jocasta Open the wine, at least.
John I'm trying to.

Buzz (continuous)

Jocasta Sorry.

Jocasta exits R

Nancy Timer?
Jocasta (*off*) Sometimes you turn it off, and two minutes later ...
Nicholas It's rather nice, the buzz.
Nancy Like bees.
John Soporific.
Nancy Summer afternoon.
Nicholas Glass of wine in front of you ...
John Turn it *off*!
Jocasta (*off*) I'm trying to!

The buzzing stops

Jocasta enters R

Jocasta I keep meaning to get the man. Sorry.
Nicholas And at least we haven't got the ——

Chink

Nancy It's some sort of creature.
Nicholas Creature?
Nancy A cricket. A frog. Some sort of tropical frog. Perhaps it was someone's pet, and it escaped. Now it's trapped somewhere.

Chink

It's getting desperate.

Chink

Nancy It's in the ceiling ...

They watch. Chink

Jocasta It's the smoke alarm.
Nancy Oh my God.
Nicholas The house is on fire.
John Except it isn't.
Nancy Is it?
Nicholas The machine says it is!
John Well, it's wrong.
Nicholas A smoke alarm must know more about smoke than you do!

John It's lying.
Nicholas That's a terrible accusation.
John There is no smoke.
Nicholas There must be smoke.
John Look!
Nicholas I don't need to look. I can hear.
Nancy I can smell burning.

They all sniff

Buzz (continuous)

Nicholas I can smell buzzing.
Jocasta Sorry.

Jocasta exits R

The buzzing stops. Chink

Nancy Perhaps it needs a new battery.
Nicholas Perhaps we need the instructions.

Jocasta enters R *carrying a drawer*

Jocasta In here somewhere. *(She dumps the contents — a mass of instruction books — on the table)*
Nicholas These are all instructions? Instructions for gadgets? You have gadgets to fit all these instructions?
John Of course not. We throw out the gadgets when they break down.
Jocasta We never throw out the instructions.
John Hair-curler ... Eyebrow-trimmer ... Toaster ...
Jocasta We don't need instructions for the toaster! *(She picks up the toaster book and puts it aside)*
John We might. *(He puts the book back in the pile)*

Chink

Nancy Perhaps it's trying to tell us it needs a new battery.
Nicholas *(picking up a book)* Electric carving knife ... You haven't got an electric carving-knife!
Jocasta We threw the electric carving-knife out ten years ago! *(She puts the book aside)*
Nicholas *(putting the book back in the main pile)* You never know. Christmas Day. In rushes the man from across the street, desperate. Turkey on the

table, fifteen people to dinner, and the carving-knife is going chink.
John (*picking up a book*) Here we are — smoke-alarm.
Jocasta Right at the bottom. The house could have burnt down by now.
Nancy I think it may just need ——
Nicholas Yes, we heard you.
Nancy — a new battery.
Nicholas Don't be silly. Things don't go ——

Chink

— to tell you they need a new battery.

John reads the instructions

John It needs a new battery.
Nicholas It needs a new battery. Obviously.
John (*to Nicholas*) Just help me ... Thanks.

John and Nicholas drag the table under the smoke alarm. John climbs on the table

Jocasta Have we got a new battery?
Nicholas Of course you haven't. But if he takes out the old battery, at least it won't keep going ——

Chink. Buzz (continuous)

Jocasta exits R

The phone rings

Jocasta enters R

Nicholas I'll get it ... (*He answers the phone*)

Jocasta exits R

(*Into the phone*) Hallo? ... No, he's dealing with the chink. ... The chink.
... Yes — he's standing on the table. Can he ...? No, OK, hold on ... (*To John*) Rather urgent.

The buzz stops

John Cordless.

Nancy Where?

Jocasta enters R, *holding a cordless phone*

Jocasta Here ...
John Thanks.
Nicholas What do I do?
John Press nine.
Nicholas (*pressing the button*) Nine.
Jocasta Not nine!
John Not nine!
Jocasta You're always doing this!
John I mean eight!
Jocasta Nine's the living-room! It's gone into the living-room now!

Jocasta heads towards the exit C

John You don't have to run after it! You can get it back, you can get it back!
Jocasta You can get it back if you can remember what to press to get it back,
    but you can never remember what to press!

Buzz (*continuous*)

    Oh, no!
Nancy Living-room? I'll go, I'll go!
John Sit down, sit down!
Nicholas They didn't pay whatever it was for this wonderful system to have
    people go running all over the house like sheep-dogs, rounding up stray
    calls.
John Just press ... What is it?

Chink

Jocasta You're going to make a mess of it, whatever you do.

Jocasta exits R

Nancy It'll just be quicker for me to ...

Nancy exits C

John Press Recall.
Nicholas (*pressing the button*) Recall.

Jocasta enters R

Jocasta No! Not Recall!
John I mean Redial!
Nicholas (*pressing the button*) Redial.
Jocasta Certainly not Redial! You'll never get it back now!
John It's that buzzer! I can't think with that buzzer going!

Chink

Nancy enters C

Nancy It stopped just as I picked it up.
Jocasta It's ringing in the bedroom now.
Nancy Bedroom, right.
Jocasta It rings each extension in turn.
Nancy Which bedroom?
John Front.
Jocasta Back.
John Front first!
Jocasta Back first!

Nancy exits C

John It doesn't matter ——
Nicholas He sounded desperate.
John — because it'll end up on the answering machine. We'll hear it on the answering machine ...

Chink

(*To Jocasta*) Buzzer, buzzer! (*To Nicholas*) We'll pick it up on the answering machine.
Jocasta You can't pick it up on the answering machine! We're always trying to pick it up on the answering machine, and you can't!
John You can if you do it from the downstairs bathroom.
Jocasta No, from the study.
John The downstairs bathroom!
Jocasta The study!

Nancy enters C

Nancy It wasn't the front bedroom ——

Jocasta No, it was the back! *Now* it's the front!
John No, *now* it's the upstairs bathroom! (*To Jocasta*) Will you stop that
   buzzing? It's driving me mad!
Nancy Upstairs bathroom?
Nicholas My turn.

Jocasta exits R

(*To Nancy*) You open the wine.

Chink

John (*to the smoke alarm*) Oh, shut up!

Nicholas exits C

Car alarm

Nicholas enters C

Nicholas Not yours?
John Or yours?
Nicholas Oh *no*, not again!

Nicholas exits L

John (*to Nancy*) Open the wine. It sounds as if he might need a drink.

Nancy picks up the wine and the corkscrew and sets to work

The buzzer stops

Jocasta enters R

Jocasta (*to Nancy*) What are you doing?
Nancy Opening the wine.
Jocasta Not with that thing!
John What do you mean, not with that thing!
Nancy I'm not very good with gadgets.
John It's *easier* with that thing!
Jocasta I'll get you an ordinary one.

Jocasta exits R

Doorbell

Nancy What's that?
John Doorbell.

Jocasta enters R

Jocasta Who on earth?
Nancy I'll go.
John *I'll* go! (*To Nancy*) Wine, wine!

John gets down from the table and exits L

Jocasta (*to Nancy*) Wait! Corkscrew!

Jocasta exits R

Voice on Answering Machine *John, it's Peter Pinch, in the accounts office ...*

John enters L

John Oh, God, it's got on the answering machine!
Voice *Sorry to call you at home, but this is a bit urgent ...*
John Get off the line, then! I'll call you back!
Voice *I gather you never pick up the phone in the evenings if it's business, but this really is a bit desperate ...*

Jocasta exits R

Voice *I'm at the office. There's a bit of a crisis on.*
Jocasta What's all this?
John I don't know!
Voice *I'm told you* are *at home this evening, so if you* could *pick it up ...*
Jocasta Pick it up, pick it up!
John Downstairs bathroom?

John exits C

Jocasta (*calling after him*) Study! Study!

Doorbell

Nancy The door ...
Jocasta *I'll* go!

Buzz (continuous)

Jocasta You do the buzzer. No, leave it, leave it.
Nancy I'll do the wine. (*She picks up the bottle and the corkscrew and sets to work*)
Jocasta No! Wait! Don't do anything!

Jocasta exits L

John enters C

John I can't! It won't! Nothing happens!
Voice *John ...? John ...? I really would be grateful if you* could *pick up the phone ...*
John (*to the answering machine*) I *have*! I've gone into the downstairs bathroom and picked it up, and it still doesn't work! (*To Nancy*) Not like that! You'll have your finger off!

John takes the bottle and the corkscrew from Nancy

Voice *John! Please!*

Nicholas and Jocasta enter L

Nicholas Not mine.
John Oh, good.
Voice *I've got the annual returns in front of me, and frankly alarm bells are ringing ...*
John (*to the answering machine*) Get off the *line*, then!
Nicholas What's all this?
John I have not the faintest notion!

Car alarm

John Oh, these bloody people and their car alarms ... And that buzzer! I'll boot that buzzer into touch for a start!

John exits R

Jocasta I'll do it!

Jocasta exits R

Nicholas Blue Renault.

John enters R

John Blue Renault?
Nicholas Isn't that yours?
John Oh, *no!*

John exits L, *with the wine and corkscrew, followed by Nicholas*

Nicholas There's glass everywhere ...

John enters L, *followed by Nicholas*

John (*handing the wine and corkscrew to Nancy*) Hold this. Don't try to do
it.
Nicholas The stereo's gone ...

John exits L, *followed by Nicholas*

Voice *.John, I realize this is probably not a good moment, but we're talking
bankruptcy ...*

John enters L

John (*stopping*) Bankruptcy? (*He calls off*) You did say *downstairs*? You
did say *downstairs* bathroom?
Jocasta (*off*) What?
Nancy No, I think she said ——
John Upstairs? She said upstairs? You pick it up from the *upstairs*
bathroom?
Nancy Well, I think she said ——

John exits C

— the study.

Jocasta enters R

Jocasta The buzzer's completely jammed ... ! What is it? What's he want?
Nancy He said was it the upstairs bathroom?

Jocasta Study! Study!
Nancy I'll tell him.
Jocasta *I'll* tell him.

The car alarm stops

  Jocasta exits C

Nancy I'll just open the ... (*She attempts to open the bottle, screams and drops it*)

  Jocasta enters C

Jocasta What, what?
Nancy I'm so sorry. I think I've ...
Jocasta Oh, no!

  Nicholas enters L

Nicholas What in heaven's name ...?
Jocasta Her finger!
Nicholas You know you can't do anything mechanical!
Jocasta Is there an artery in your finger?
Nancy I'm fine, I'm fine.
Nicholas Hold it up in the air ... You're getting blood over everything!
Jocasta Tourniquet ...
Nicholas Teacloth!
Nancy Don't fuss, I'm fine.
Nicholas No, but it's going everywhere! Newspaper! I'm so sorry about this.
Jocasta Casualty! Get her to casualty!
Nancy I just feel a bit faint ...
Jocasta Casualty! Casualty!

Jocasta and Nicholas hustle Nancy away to the L

Nicholas I'm so sorry.
Nancy I think I *did* get it open. I think it's pouring over the carpet.
Jocasta (*calling*) John! *John...*! Leave that! Emergency!
Nicholas *I'll* tell him! You get her into the car!

  Nicholas exits C

Jocasta (*calling after Nicholas*) He's in the upstairs bathroom!

Jocasta rushes Nancy off L *during the next line*

Jocasta (*to Nancy*) Keep calm! There's nothing to worry about!

   They exit

   John enters C

John I *knew* you couldn't do it from the upstairs bathroom! Where are you ...? Where is everybody?
Voice *I don't want to panic you, John, but do you know the kind of sentences that judges are handing out now for fraud ...?*

   Jocasta and Nancy enter L

Jocasta Doorkeys! Haven't got my doorkeys!
John What in heaven's name ...?
Jocasta Bleeding! Bottle! Finger! Casualty!
John Oh, my God!
Jocasta Car! Get her into the car!

   John rushes Nancy off L

   Doorkeys!

   Jocasta exits R

   John and Nancy enter L

John Car! Broken glass!

   Jocasta enters R

Jocasta Their car!
John Their car.

   John and Nancy exit L

Jocasta What was I doing ...? Doorkeys!

   Jocasta exits R

   Nicholas enters C

Nicholas Not in the upstairs bathroom ... You didn't say the *study*? You didn't say the *attic* ...?

Nicholas exits C

John and Nancy enter

John Doorkeys! Haven't got the doorkeys!
Nancy I think I'm going to faint.
John Car! Car! Get in the car!

Nancy remains where she is, dazed

Jocasta enters R

John Doorkeys!
Jocasta Doorkeys!
John On the hook!

John exits R

Jocasta (*calling after John*) Not on the hook!
Nancy I'm so sorry ...
Jocasta (*to Nancy*) In the car! (*She calls after John*) I've just looked!

Jocasta exits R

Nancy I don't think I can quite ... (*She sits down and puts her head between her knees*)

The buzzer stops

John enters R, *with a large cast-iron saucepan*

John (*after Jocasta*) Not on the hook!

Jocasta enters R

Jocasta I *said* — not on the ... (*She sees the saucepan*)
John Table.
Jocasta Saucepan?
John Buzzer. Fixed the buzzer. Table!
Jocasta Table?

John (*searching*) Doorkeys! On the table ...! Under the table! Move the table! (*He puts the saucepan down on the table and, with a struggle, drags the table back into its original position, where it conceals Nancy, whom he does not notice*) Doing the thing! With the doorkeys! Put them down! Fell on the floor!

No sign of them there

Nicholas enters C

Nicholas Not in the study.
John The doorkeys?
Nicholas You.
John Me?
Nicholas Looking for you.
John I'm here.
Nicholas Slight problem with the ——
John I know!
Nicholas Where is she?
John In the car!
Nicholas In the car?
Jocasta (*to Nicholas*) In the car!
Nicholas In the car ...

Nicholas exits L

Jocasta Try the bedroom!
John The bedroom?

John exits C

Nicholas enters L

Nicholas The bedroom?
Jocasta (*calling after John*) By the bed! On the bed!
Nicholas On the *bed*?
Jocasta (*to John*) *Under* the bed!
Nicholas *Under* the bed?

Nicholas heads for the exit C

Jocasta (*to Nicholas*) The keys! Her? In the car!
Nicholas In the car ...

Nicholas exits L

John enters C, *waving doorkeys*

John By the phone!
Jocasta In the car!
John In the car! Burglar-alarm!
Jocasta Burglar-alarm!

John and Jocasta move L. *John stops by the entrance* L. *The burglar-alarm is deemed to be just off* L *so we cannot see it, but can see whoever operates it*

Jocasta exits L

Voice *Three years, John — five years ...!*

John sets the alarm. We hear four pips followed by a warbling tone

John moves further into the room

John Five years?
Nicholas (*off*) She's not in the car!

Nicholas enters L

Nicholas Where is she?

Jocasta enters L

Jocasta She's in the car!
Nicholas She's not in the car!
John Five years!
Jocasta Alarm, alarm!

Jocasta bundles John and Nicholas off L

There is the sound of the front door slamming, then a continuous tone from the burglar alarm

Voice *Come on! You can't simply hide under the table!*

Nancy sits up groggily from behind the table

Nancy Sorry.
Jocasta (*off*) Keys! Keys! Who's got the keys?
John (*off*) I've got the keys!

There is the sound of the front door opening

The continuous tone from the burglar alarm turns to an urgent interrupted warning tone

Nancy subsides behind the table again

   Jocasta, Nicholas and John enter L

Jocasta (*calling*) Nancy!
John (*calling*) Nancy!
Jocasta I thought she was in the car!
Nicholas I told you she wasn't in the car!
Jocasta (*calling*) Nancy!
John Alarm!
Jocasta Alarm ... (*She moves to the alarm and operates it*)

There are four pips as the burglar alarm is disarmed

John (*calls*) Nancy!

   John exits R, *searching*

Nancy (*sitting up again*) Sorry. I can't quite ... (*She disappears behind the table again*)
Nicholas What on earth ...? (*He drags the table out of the way*)

Jocasta moves further into the room

Jocasta What on earth ...?
Nicholas Under the table!

Jocasta and Nicholas rush Nancy L. *Jocasta operates the alarm*

We hear four pips, followed by a warbling tone

   Jocasta, Nicholas and Nancy exit

   John enters R

John Lights, lights ...

John exits R *to switch off the kitchen lights*

We hear the slam of the front door, L, *and the continuous tone from the burglar alarm*

John enters R

John Hold on, hold on! I'm still inside! (*He runs towards the burglar alarm, but gets his foot stuck in the saucepan*)

The continuous tone goes on

Jocasta (*off*) John, where are you? What are you playing at?

We hear Jocasta hammering on the front door

It's going to go off!
John I know, I know! (*He punches in digits, struggling to get the saucepan off his foot*)

The continuous tone continues

Jocasta (*off*) What's happening? I haven't got any keys!
John (*calling*) Nine-four-two-three ... It doesn't work!
Jocasta (*off*) We changed it, we changed it!
John We changed it? What to?
Jocasta (*off*) What?
John What did we change it *to*?
Jocasta (*off*) *Two*? No, *four*!
John (*punching a button*) Four *what*?
Jocasta Four nothing!
John (*punching buttons*) Four nothing ...
Voice *Come on, John — pick it up!*
John Oh, not you, *too*! (*He whirls round on the answering machine and smashes the saucepan down on to the table next to it, then turns back to the alarm*)
Jocasta (*off, screaming*) No! No two! Four! Four four four four!
John (*screaming*) But *what* four?
Jocasta (*off*) What?
John What ... *four*?
Voice *What* for? *Well, I'll explain, now you've been kind enough to answer.*

John I don't believe it! I'm *through*! (*He looks at the wonder-working saucepan, then back at the answering machine*)

Voice *Well, yes, I think you may be, because according to the computer we have a shortfall in the petty cash account of ninety-seven million pounds. So, John, before I call the police, I'd just like to hear* your *side of the story.*

John (*bitterly*) I'll tell you *my* side of the story ...

The burglar alarm goes off, together with the doorbell, car alarm, approaching police siren, etc., and, off stage, Jocasta, Nicholas and Nancy attempt to scream the number to John

John sits down quietly and puts the saucepan over his head

CURTAIN

DOUBLES

Two hotel rooms

The set consists of two standard small hotel double bedrooms, arranged so that they are mirror images of each other. US *in each room is the door to the corridor. Beside the doors are boxed-off shower/toilets, back to back against the party wall. There are double beds, also back to back against the party wall; each has bedside tables with lamps to each side. The party wall itself is notional, with a full-length mirror set into it, indicated notionally by its frame, between the bed and the window. Along the opposite wall of each bedroom is the same array of standard equipment: TV, with the screen facing* US; *a fitted wall unit that includes a luggage stand, hanging space, and built-in desk with a practical lamp; a mini-bar; an electric kettle; and a trouser-press. Each room has a notional balcony* DS, *reached by a notional door in the "fourth wall"*

LEFTHAND ROOM	RIGHTHAND ROOM
When the play begins, the room is in darkness	*When the play begins, the room is in darkness*

The US *door opens to reveal Miles, carrying an overnight bag and other travel impedimenta*

As this happens, the Lights come up

Miles stops uneasily

Miles This room ...

Melanie enters behind Miles, also carrying bags and coats

Melanie (*anxiously*) Is it all right?
Miles (*eerily*) There's something familiar about it ...
Melanie It looks all right.

Miles (*dumping his bag on the bed*) TV ... Mini-bar ... Have we somehow — gone back in time to the hotel we stayed in last night? Look — it's the same balcony! It's the same view over the hotel car-park!

Melanie (*matter-of-fact*) What about the bathroom?

Melanie exits into the bathroom

The bathroom Lights come on

Miles Yes! The bathroom's different. Last night it was here. (*He indicates the lefthand wall by the window*) Is it the hotel we stayed in the night *before* last? Or have we — strayed *forward* in time to the hotel we're going to be staying in tomorrow night?

The bathroom Lights go off

Melanie enters from the bathroom

Melanie I wish you wouldn't put your suitcase on the bed. (*She unpacks during the following*)

Miles We must write to the Good Hotel Guide. "One satisfied couple were specially struck by the charming sense of déjà-vu about the complimentary tea-bags and sterilized milk."

Melanie (*tensely*) Miles ...

Miles (*attentively*) Melanie ...

Melanie It's quite tiring, being on holiday.

Miles Exhausting.

Melanie So could we perhaps — have a little rest?

Miles We *are* having a little rest.
That's what's so exhausting.
Melanie From the jokes. Would
you mind?

*Pause. Melanie lays out her stuff on
the* DS *side of the bed. Miles feels the
party wall*

Miles Actually this particular
pattern of brown stains down the
wallpaper we *haven't* seen before.
Melanie Miles!
Miles Sorry.

Pause

(*Reading a notice on the party
wall*) "Our esteemed guests ..."

Melanie stiffens

No, but it's translated into the
most beautiful English.
Melanie Aren't you going to
unpack?
Miles (*reading*) " ... are advised
that chuckout time is noon."
Melanie Why don't you press your
trousers?
Miles Why don't I what?
Melanie There's a trouser-press.
Miles Good God, we haven't had
a trouser-press before! I shall
always think of this as "The Place
with the Trouser-press".
Melanie Sit down, then. Read a
book, or something. (*She comes
downstage and inspects herself
in the full-length mirror*)
Miles Read a book? All right. (*He
picks up the directory again*)
"Why not relax over a pre-dinner
cocktail in the intimate
atmosphere of the Commodore's
Cabin?"

Melanie To yourself! (*She goes on
inspecting herself, dissatisfied,
in the mirror, during the
following*)

*Miles watches Melanie, then turns
back to the directory*

Miles (*reading*) "As you sip you
can study the choice of specially
selected local and international
dishes in our celebrated
Downtowner Dining-room and
Groll."
Melanie At least take your suitcase
off the bed.
Miles (*moving his suitcase on to
the floor beside the TV*) When
you think of them all, though. All
the people who've been in this
room before us. Unpacked their
bags. (*He opens his suitcase*)
Packed them up again. Thrown
their complimentary cups of tea
at the wall. Three hundred and
sixty-seven couples a year. They
come through the door. They look
round. She checks the bathroom.
He reads out the funny English.
Together they discover the
complimentary trouser-press ...
Melanie I'm going to have a
shower.

Melanie retires into the bathroom

The bathroom Lights come on

*Miles sinks down on the bed,
suddenly gloomy. He attempts to
unpack during the following*

And then you think—how many
rooms are there in the hotel? Two

hundred? Three hundred? So every night three hundred doors are opening, and three hundred couples are coming in, and looking round, and reading out about the chuckout time and the Groll, and discovering the trouser-press ... So that's one hundred thousand couples a year ... Ten thousand hotels, all the same ... A thousand million couples. Every couple having the same experiences ... All turning into the same couple, repeated a thousand million times ... (*He gives up his attempt at unpacking, overcome with gloom*)

The US *door opens to reveal Laurence, carrying an overnight bag and other travel impedimenta*

As this happens, the Lights come up

Laurence looks around the room

Laurence Trouser-press. (*He advances into the room*)

Lynn enters, also carrying bags and coats, and follows Laurence

Trouser-press, look. (*He investigates the room's equipment during the following*)
Lynn So I see.
Laurence What?
Lynn Nothing.
Laurence Don't like it?
Lynn Lovely.
Laurence No different from the one last night.
Lynn Or the night before.
Laurence You liked them.

Lynn Did I?

Laurence It's only for one night.

Lynn (*looking at the party wall*) Some sort of brown stuff spilt down the wall.

Laurence Well, that makes a change.

Lynn Very distinctive.

Laurence Come on! We'll be somewhere else tomorrow night.

Lynn I know. Somewhere like this.

Laurence Balcony. Nice view.

Lynn It's the hotel car-park.

Laurence It could be the gasworks.

Lynn You can keep an eye on the car.

Laurence Give it a rest.

Lynn That's all you worry about.

Laurence Cup of tea?

Lynn No, thanks.

Laurence Kettle. All the doings.

Lynn I don't want one!

Laurence Mini-bar ... You want a drink?

Lynn What's the bathroom like?

Lynn goes into the bathroom. The bathroom Lights come on

Laurence goes on inspecting the equipment of the room

Laurence Biscuits ... Biscuits ... More biscuits ...

The Lights go off in the bathroom

Lynn comes out of the bathroom

Lynn It's sanitized for our personal protection.

Laurence Good. No shortage of biscuits!

Lynn We've got our own biscuits.

Laurence Well, now we've got some spare ones. (*He lays out his stuff on the* US *side of the bed during the following*) I'll go this side, OK?

Lynn What are you asking for?

Laurence Go the other way round if you like. We're on holiday.

Lynn (*reading a notice on the party wall*)"Our esteemed guests are advised that chuckout time is noon."

Laurence Noon? Right.

Lynn Chuckout time.

Laurence Aren't you going to unpack? (*He continues unpacking*)

Lynn picks up the directory of hotel services on the desk

Lynn (*reading*) "Why not relax over a pre-dinner cocktail in the intimate atmosphere of the Commodore's Cabin?"

Laurence Have a drink here if you want one.

Lynn (*reading*) "As you sip you can study the choice of specially selected local and international dishes in our celebrated Downtowner Dining-room and Groll."

Laurence Do you want a drink or don't you?

Lynn I want a nice grolled steak. Medium rear. With chaps and poos.

Laurence Don't go mad. You'll be up all night again. (*He takes his trousers off*)

Lynn What — pressing your trousers?

Laurence Why not? While we've got the chance? (*He puts his trousers in the press*)

Lynn (*watching Laurence gloomily*) Funny, when you think there was someone else taking off his trousers in here last night. (*She comes* DS *and looks at herself in the notional full-length mirror on the party wall between the bed and the window*) Someone else in that mirror. Looking back at themselves.

Laurence Moaning away about everything.

Lynn Someone else the night before that. Someone else tomorrow night. Someone on the other side of the wall ... (*She sinks down on to the bed, overcome by melancholy*)

Laurence (*inspecting his bare legs*) Might as well have a crap, now I've got them off.

Laurence exits into the bathroom

The bathroom Lights come on

Miles (*calling*) Shall I come and scrub your back ...?

Lynn (*calling*) What?

Shall I come and work on various parts of you?

What are you mumbling about?

Melanie (*off*) What?

Miles I said ... Oh, never mind.

Laurence (*off*) What?
Lynn I said ... Oh, never mind.

Miles turns on the TV. There is the sound of an announcer reading a news bulletin in Rewindese, the language a recording makes when it's run backwards. Miles watches gloomily for a few moments, then presses the remote, and the news is replaced by the sounds of a Rewindese love scene

Lynn turns on the TV. There is the sound of an announcer reading a news bulletin in Rewindese, the language a recording makes when it's run backwards. Lynn watches gloomily for a few moments, then presses the remote, and the news is replaced by he sounds of a Rewindese love scene

The bathroom Lights go off

The bathroom Lights go off

Melanie, in a dressing-gown, enters from the bathroom

Laurence enters, still trouserless, from the bathroom

Melanie Miles, you're not going to leave your bag there?

Laurence Changed my mind.

Miles instantaneously switches back to the news. Pause. He becomes aware of Melanie

Lynn instantaneously switches back to the news. Pause. She becomes aware of Laurence

Miles What?

Lynn What?

Pause

Pause

Melanie What are you watching?
Miles No idea.

Laurence What's all this, then?
Lynn Search me.

Melanie What's it about?
Miles Shortfall in self-adhesive envelope production.

Laurence Where's the whatsit?

Melanie Try the other channels.

Melanie picks up the TV remote and presses the button

Laurence picks up the TV remote and presses the button

We hear the love scene

We hear the love scene

Oh dear.

Melanie gazes at the screen, in spite of herself

Oh dear oh dear. (*He gazes at the screen in spite of himself*)
Lynn (*gazing too*) She's trying to tell him something.

Miles (*also gazing*) She's trying to tell him she reversed the car into a bollard.

Laurence We don't want to watch this kind of thing, do we?

Melanie switches the TV off

Laurence switches the TV off

Miles Oh.
Melanie Somebody's going to fall over that bag.
Miles Me.
Melanie Probably. It was you last night.
Miles And the night before.

Lynn Oh.

Miles puts his hand under Melanie's dressing-gown

Lynn puts her hand on Laurence's bare knee

Melanie (*startled*) What?

Laurence (*baffled*) What?
Lynn Since you've got your trousers off already...

Miles Another letter to the Good Hotel Guide. "One guest complained about the shocking flimsiness of his partner's underwear."

Laurence They should be done by now.

Melanie (*pushing Miles's hand away*) I've had my shower. (*She gets dressed during the following*)

Miles inspects himself gloomily in the full-length mirror, turning his head this way and that

Aren't you going to change?
Miles I have. Out of all recognition.

.
I never used to look like that.
Melanie I thought we were going to eat?

They'll have stopped serving.

Miles puts his face very close to the mirror, and contorts it as he examines it

But is that really me?

Or is that some complete stranger gazing back at me?

Melanie holds up a pair of trousers and examines them

Melanie Got a bit crumpled. (*She puts the trousers on*)

Miles glances round

Miles Perfect. (*He turns back to the mirror*)

Laurence inspects the trouser-press. Lynn inspects herself gloomily in the full-length mirror, turning her head this way and that

Lynn I don't look like that, do I?

Laurence We eating, or what?
Lynn Do something to my face.

Lynn fetches her handbag and makes up her face in the mirror during the following, putting her face very close to the mirror, and contorting it

I still look like me if I put a bit of make-up on, don't I?

Laurence holds up the pressed trousers

Laurence How about that?

Lynn glances round

Wonderful.

Lynn turns back to the mirror

I suppose I'm talking to myself.

(To his image) Hallo!

What's it like in there?

You're trying to say something.

I didn't quite catch what you said.

You always speak at exactly the same time as I do!

Melanie joins Miles at the mirror, to inspect the effect of her trousers

Melanie What do you think?

Miles I said — perfect.

Melanie Not *too* creased?
Miles Wonderful.

Come here.

Melanie moves to Miles

Miles indicates their image in the mirror

I suppose I'm talking to myself.
(To her image) Hallo!

How are *you* today?

Did you say something?

What was that?

The trouble is ...

You always speak at exactly the same time as I do!

Laurence joins Lynn at the mirror, to inspect the effect of his trousers

Laurence All right?

Lynn I said — wonderful.
Laurence Not *too* creased?

Lynn Perfect.

Look.

Lynn indicates their image in the mirror

That's us.

That's us.
Laurence I know.

What do you think?
Melanie What do I think?

Lynn Are we — all right?
Laurence Are we all right?

Miles Are we convincing?

Why, what's wrong?

Melanie They *are* a bit creased.

Lynn I just sometimes wish ...

Miles Because I sometimes feel ...

Pause

Pause

I don't know ...

Never mind.
Melanie Come on.

Laurence I'm starving.

Laurence moves Lynn towards the door

Melanie moves Miles towards the door

Miles Melanie, Melanie ...

Lynn Come back.

Lynn drags Laurence back to the mirror

Miles drags Melanie back to the mirror

I'll tell you something surprising ...

Just suppose ...

That's not us ...

... that wasn't us.

Because that's not a mirror ...

That's a window ...

So that's not our room ...

We're looking into the next room ...

It's just like this one ...

All the same things ...

Bed, look ...

Trouser-press.

And then suddenly ...

There in the middle of it all ...

These two.

Who are they?

Two complete strangers.

Never seen them before in our lives.

Look at them ...

Funny looking pair.
Laurence Don't look funny to me.

Melanie We did stop the papers?
Miles No, but what do we think?

Lynn Are they nice? Are they nasty?

Sort of people we want to know?

Laurence You've got a funny way of looking at things, my pet.

Melanie You always want to see
things differently from other
people.

Laurence Come on.

Miles No, but ——
Melanie Dinner.

Eat.

They move towards the door

*They move towards the door. Lynn
stops*

Laurence Now what?
Lynn Just thinking.
Laurence Just thinking what?
Lynn What's going to be happening
when we're not here?
Laurence What?

Miles stops

Miles You know what's going to
be going on in here while we're
out?
Melanie No?
Miles No, nor do I.
Melanie What are you talking
about?

Lynn No-one pressing their
trousers.

Miles No-one reading the notices.

Melanie opens the door

Laurence opens the door

Laurence Right, off we go.

Melanie I'm going.

Lynn No-one looking at
themselves in the mirror.

Miles No-one looking at anything.

So what'll be happening?

Nothing will be happening.

Nothing at all.

Melanie (*to Laurence*) Good-
evening!

Laurence (*to Melanie*) Oh —
hallo!

(*To Miles*) Come on. I don't want
to stand there in the corridor all
evening.

(*To Lynn*) Buck up. There's
people out here waiting to come
by.

Miles Not even anything existing ...

Lynn Nothing ...

*Miles shudders, switches off the
Lights, and goes out. The door
closes*

*Lynn shudders, switches off the
lights, and exits. The door closes*

Darkness

Darkness

*The door immediately re-opens,
and Miles enters*

The Lights come up again

Miles looks round the room

Melanie enters

Melanie What in heaven's name is
it now?
Miles Just checking.
Melanie Checking what?

Miles That it's all still here.
Melanie (*coldly*) Oh, and is it?
Miles It saw me coming.

Miles ushers Melanie out, and switches off the Lights. The door closes

Darkness. Music for a moment

Melanie opens the door; Miles is with her

The bedside Lights come up

Melanie (*politely*) Good-night!

Miles (*politely*) Good-night!

Melanie comes in, switching on the main lights. Miles follows, closing the door

Miles Kevin and Sharon!

The original Kevin and Sharon! (*He flings himself down on the bed*)

Why is it that one's fellow-countrymen abroad are so embarrassing?

Music for a moment

Laurence opens the door; Lynn is with him

The bedside lights come up

Laurence (*genially*) 'Night 'night, then!

Lynn (*genially*) Sleep tight!

Laurence enters, switching on the main lights. Lynn follows, closing the door

Laurence What a Nigel!

Nigel and Nigella!

Nigel and Nigella Prat!

Kind of people who make you feel ashamed to be British.

Melanie Do you want the
bathroom?
Miles "After you, Sharon." "Oh, ta
ever so, Kevvy."

Melanie exits into the bathroom

The Lights come on

Lynn At least they were saying
something to each other. At least
they weren't sitting there in total
silence.

Lynn exits into the bathroom

The bathroom lights come on

Laurence (*undressing*) No — he
never stopped! Voice you can
hear half-way across the
restaurant. Snigger, snigger,
snigger, about everything.
Something funny about the
music, something funny about
the tablecloths. Soup doesn't
come up to his high standards.
They've done something comic
with the fish. I thought we were
never going to hear the last of the
sweet trolley. And he thinks *he's*
not comic? He's the comicest
thing of the lot! All this sniffing
the wine, all this swilling it round.
You hear what he said? "Full and
fruity, with just a hint of moles'
armpits."

The lavatory flushes

*Melanie comes out of the
bathroom to fetch something*

Miles I think they're talking about
  us. Kevin and Sharon. I can hear
  a low indignant burbling coming
  through the wall.
Melanie His name's Laurence.
Miles Laurence?
Melanie She called him Laurence.
Miles Laurence ...
Melanie Nothing funny about
  being called Laurence, is there?

Melanie exits into the bathroom

Melanie Nothing at all. Wonderful
  name. Saint Laurence. Lawrence
  of Arabia ... What's she called?
Melanie (*off*) Lynn.
Miles Lynn? Did you say Lynn?
  Laurence and *Lynn*?

The lavatory flushes

Lynn comes out of the bathroom

Lynn What?
Laurence What?
Lynn I thought you said something.
Laurence I did. I said, "Full and
  fruity, with just a hint of old
  jockstraps."

Lynn exits into the bathroom

*Melanie enters from the
bathroom*

Melanie I should keep your voice
  down.
Miles They can't hear.
Melanie I can hear *them*.
Miles What, in the bathroom? You
  mean having a pee?

*Melanie goes back into the
bathroom*

Or worse? All right, I don't want to embarrass them. I'll call them Kevin and Sharon. I don't know how you heard they were called Laurence and Lynn. They scarcely said a word all the way through dinner. Just sat there avoiding each other's eye.

The bathroom Lights go off

Melanie comes out of the bathroom and undresses during the following

Melanie Yes, because they knew you were looking at them.
Miles I wasn't looking at them.
Melanie You obviously were.
Miles I was listening to them.
Melanie You can't have been listening to them, because you were talking all the time.
Miles *You* were listening to them.
Melanie *I* wasn't listening to them.
Miles You must have been listening to them — you heard them say something to each other. "Oh, Laurence!" "Oh, Lynn!" A conversation which passed me by completely, even though I was straining my ears.
Melanie She said, "Laurence, do you want coffee?"
Miles Oh, how romantic. I'm sorry I missed that. And he replied, "Oh, no, Lynn, no coffee for me, my precious. All I want is you."
Melanie Aren't you going to get undressed?
Miles Ooh, Sharon, you saucy piece! I'll clean my teeth ever so quick!

The bathroom lights go off

Miles goes into the bathroom

The bathroom Lights come on

Lynn enters from the bathroom

Laurence "Full and fruity, with just a hint of ponces' arseholes."

Lynn He was making a joke.

Laurence Oh, really?

Lynn It's what it said in the wine-list.

Laurence "Just a hint of raspberries." I know, he read it out. Twice.

Lynn Have you cleaned your teeth?

Laurence He read out most of the wine-list.

Laurence exits into the bathroom

The bathroom Lights come on

Lynn I thought it was quite funny.

Laurence (*off*) I know. I saw you laugh.

Lynn I didn't laugh.

Laurence (*off*) *He* saw you laugh.

Lynn I didn't laugh!

Laurence (*off*) He was doing it for your benefit!

The lavatory flushes

Melanie gets into bed

Melanie I thought they were a rather sweet couple. I don't know why you have to keep putting everyone down.

Lynn I don't know why you're so cross if anything makes me laugh. I thought they seemed a nice couple.

At least he didn't keep talking all the time, he didn't keep making jokes. They could just sit there in peace.

I don't know why you can't just quietly enjoy things for a moment.

At least he was saying something. At least he was making a few jokes. They could sit there and have a good time together.

Lynn gets into bed

I wish *you'd* got a bit more sense of humour.

Laurence comes out of the bathroom, cleaning his teeth

Laurence You telling me I haven't got a sense of humour?

Lynn Well, you're not a *great* one for jokes, arc you?

Laurence Jokes? You want jokes? There's this feller goes into a bar ——

Lynn Stop cleaning your teeth for a moment, then.

Laurence There's this feller goes into a bar. Right?

Lynn Right.

Laurence No, there's this feller sitting in a bar, and this feller comes in, this other feller.

Lynn Why don't you have a little practice on your own first?

Laurence Feller walks up the wall, right? Feller who's come in. Feller watches him. Feller in the bar. Feller walks across the ceiling. OK? Walks down the other wall and out of the bar. Feller in the bar says: "That's funny, he didn't say 'Good-evening'."

The bathroom Lights go off

Miles comes out of the bathroom

Miles The imagination boggles at what old Kevin's up to in that bathroom.
Melanie What are you talking about?
Miles Cleans his teeth, then flushes the loo. I know people get a little confused about the functions of the *bidet*, but cleaning your teeth in the lavatory ...

Miles undresses during the following

Melanie Will you do something?
Miles What do you want?
Melanie We're on holiday.
Miles Yes?
Melanie Special treat. For me.
Miles OK.
Melanie Say something serious.
Miles All right.
Melanie Just one thing.
Miles One thing ... Anything?
Melanie Anything.
Miles Bright's Disease.
Melanie Thank you.

Miles gets into bed

Miles I expect old Kevin's being serious.

Lynn You've got toothpaste on your chin.
Laurence The *barman* says: "That's funny, he didn't say 'Good evening'."
Lynn Have you flushed?

Laurence goes back into the bathroom. The lavatory flushes

Laurence comes out of the bathroom

Laurence *Dog* walks into a bar——
Lynn Light.
Laurence Says to the barman——
Lynn Light. In the bathroom. It's on.

Laurence goes back into the bathroom, turns out the bathroom light and returns

Laurence You'd better move in with Nigel, then. I expect *he's* telling jokes. (*He puts his ear to the wall*)

Miles Gone very quiet in there. (*He puts his ear to the wall*)
Melanie What are you doing?

Lynn What are you doing?
Laurence (*voice down*) No-one saying anything at all in there, I'll tell you that.

Miles (*lowering his voice*) Bit of serious whispering going on.

Bit of whispering, that's all.

Lynn I don't think that's very nice.

Melanie That's a horrible thing to do.
Miles Sh!
He's saying something ...

Laurence Sh!

What's he saying?

"Oh, Sharon, I love you!"

He takes his head away from the wall and gazes at it in mock surprise

Laurence takes his head away from the wall and gazes at the wall in surprise

Lynn What?

Miles reapplies his ear to the wall

Laurence reapplies his ear to the wall

"Oh, Kevin, I love you, too!"

He starts away from the wall again in mock surprise

He starts away from the wall again. He laughs

What? What's going on?
Laurence No sense of humour? What about this, then? Old Nigel and Nigella in there ...

Miles puts his ear back to the wall, and starts away again in genuine surprise

Laurence laughs

Good God.
Melanie Why? What's happening?
Miles (*disconcerted*) Laughing his head off.

Lynn What? What?
Laurence Know what they're called? Kevin and Sharon!

Miles turns out the main lights and side lights

Laurence turns out the main lights and the side lights

Darkness

Darkness

There is a pause

Miles's side light comes on again. Miles is sitting up in bed, looking round the room

Melanie Now what?
Miles Just checking. (*He turns his light out again*)

Darkness

Laurence Kevin and Sharon!

Lynn Very funny.

Laurence All right — tell you something else, then.

Lynn No more jokes tonight.

Laurence No, something serious.

Lynn Bit of sleep first.

Pause

Laurence I love you.

Pause

   I said I love you.

Lynn Um.

Pause

Miles You know I love you?

Melanie (*coolly*) Do you?

Miles You know I do. It's the Kevin and Sharon story all over again.

Melanie Oh.

Miles No, I'm saying something serious. I'm trying to say something serious. I *am* saying something serious.

Melanie Oh, good.

Miles So how about you?

Melanie What?

Miles Do you love me?

Melanie Yes.

Miles Yes?

Melanie I've said — yes!

Miles's side light comes on

   Now what?

Miles Just checking.

Melanie Do stop this!

Miles No, the expression on your face when you say that.

Melanie turns out the light

Lynn Laurence? You're not asleep, are you?
Laurence Um?
Lynn Laurence ...
Laurence What's the matter?
Lynn I love you, too.

Pause

Lynn's sidelight comes on. Lynn is sitting up in bed

Laurence What? I said! I said before!
Lynn Mosquito.
Laurence Mosquito?
Lynn I heard it.
Laurence I can't hear anything.
Lynn I heard it!
Laurence Gone.
Lynn It'll be back.
Laurence Get some sleep.
Lynn Soon as we put the lights out. (*She puts the light out*)
Laurence Not a sound.
Lynn I'm listening.
Laurence Go to sleep.
Lynn I'm waiting.

Miles's side light comes on. Miles is sitting up in bed looking at Melanie

Miles "Yes?" Just — "yes"?
Melanie What are you talking about?
Miles I say, "Do you love me?" And you just say "Yes", and turn out the lights?

*There is a pause. Then Melanie
turns over and embraces Miles*

Melanie Come on, then.
Miles I didn't mean that.
Melanie Yes, you did. Come on.
   Quietly, though.
Miles Quietly, right.
Melanie Don't wake the whole
   hotel.
Miles Don't want to make Kevin
   and Sharon jealous.

*Lynn's side light comes on. Lynn is
sitting up in bed, slapping at herself*

Lynn Get off! Get off!
Laurence What, back?
Lynn I felt it go in! Look, blood!
   There's blood on the sheet!

Miles Oh, dear. Bit of competition.
Melanie Never mind them. Go on
   if you're going to.

There! There! (*She jumps up on
the bed, pointing at the ceiling,
and pulls the duvet round her*)
Laurence (*getting to his feet*)
   Where?
Lynn There!

*Laurence reaches into the bath-
room for a towel and attempts to
track the mosquito as it moves about
the room*

Up here ... ! Down there ... ! No ...
Yes!
Laurence Oh, right ... You little
   devil! (*He enters into the spirit of
   the chase*)
Lynn Give me another towel ...

*Laurence grabs another towel and
hands it to Lynn*

Laurence Here! (*He slaps his tow-
el at the mosquito*)
Lynn There! (*She slaps*)
Laurence Where?

They rain a fusillade of slaps

Miles What — flagellation?
Melanie Don't listen.
Miles Don't listen?

Lynn Nearly!
Laurence Wor!
Lynn Careful!
Laurence Wallop! Wallop!
Lynn Wait, wait ... Now!
Laurence Ah!
Lynn Yes! No ...

They pause, panting, searching

Miles We should have guessed.
  They look so abnormally
  normal ...
Melanie They've finished.
Miles Have they?
Melanie Go on.
Miles I'm listening.
Melanie Silence.
Miles Right ...

*They both cry out, pointing at the
ceiling over the bed. They jump
wildly about all over the bed, grunt-
ing and shouting, trying to reach
the mosquito as it moves around
the ceiling*

Laurence Gotcher!
Lynn Gotcher!
Laurence Very satisfactory.

Lynn That's my blood on the ceiling.

They settle down in bed

Laurence Know what?
Lynn What?
Laurence I enjoyed that.

Miles reaches for the light switch on his bedside light

Melanie No?
Miles No.

Miles turns out the Light

Laurence turns out the Light

Music plays, as before

Music plays, as before

During the following Miles gets out of bed, moves across the room and falls to his knees in his suitcase

We hear the crash of a table-lamp on the desk falling over

Melanie (*sleepily*) What's happening?
Miles Nothing. Go back to sleep.
Melanie Turn on the light.
Miles That *was* the light.

There are more noises in the darkness

Melanie What time is it?
Miles Quarter past three.
Melanie What are you doing?
Miles Trying not to disturb you.

There is a pause, then a crash, a cry of pain from Miles, and the noise of a gunfight, very loud, dramatic music and shouts in Rewindese

Melanie Oh, my God!

She turns on her side light

Laurence turns on his side light

Laurence There's a riot going on!

Miles is on his hands and knees in his suitcase. The table lamp on his side of the bed is now on the floor

Melanie What in the name of heaven ...?
Miles Suitcase!

Not the car? They're not attacking the car? (*He jumps out of bed and hurries to the window to look*)

Melanie You've turned the TV on!
Miles I fell on the remote!
Melanie Turn it off!
Miles I'm trying to! I can't find it!
Melanie You'll wake the whole hotel!

Lynn It's next door! They've gone mad! (*She hammers on the wall*)

It's next door! You've woken them up!
Miles (*hunting through spilled clothes*) I can't find the remote!

You'll have to go and talk to them!

Laurence storms out of the door, followed by Lynn

Melanie What's this? (*She retrieves the remote*)

Miles That's it!

*There is a thundering on the door.
Miles moves to open it*

Melanie Which button?
Miles The top one!

*Melanie presses a button. The TV
sound redoubles in intensity*

Miles opens the door

    *Laurence stands on the threshold,
with Lynn behind him*

Laurence Look, I'm sorry, but it's
   three o'clock in the morning ...!
Miles I know, I know! (*To Melanie*)
   The top one, the top one!

*Melanie presses the button again.
The TV sound redoubles in intensity
again*

*Miles hurries back to help Melanie,
followed by Laurence and Lynn*

    The bottom one!

*Melanie presses another button.
The sound switches to low-grade
Rewindese porn, hugely loud*

    Oh, my God ... ! The blue one!
    The red one!
Lynn (*screaming*) The one that
   says "off!"

*Melanie presses another button.
Silence*

There is a pause

Miles I'm so sorry.
Laurence I thought we'd got a riot
    going on!
Miles I am most abjectly apologetic.
Lynn He thought it was the car! He
    thought they'd got the cars!
Miles I fell on the remote. I do most
    humbly and contritely apologize.
Melanie But — what were you
    doing?
Miles I was trying not to disturb
    you.
Melanie I know. But ...
Miles Looking for the bathroom.
    (*He feels along the* DL *wall to
    demonstrate*) Couldn't find the
    door.
Melanie The bathroom's over here!
    (*She points to it,* US)

*Miles looks at the bathroom, then
back at the* DL *wall*

Miles It was here last night.
Laurence Well, if you're OK ...

*Laurence and Lynn execute a
withdrawal*

Melanie I'm terribly sorry.
Miles Extremely sorry.
Lynn No, sorry to come bursting
    in.
Melanie Very sorry.
Laurence No, only it's three
    o'clock in the morning ...
Melanie Dreadfully sorry.

Laurence and Lynn exit

*Miles closes the door. There is a
pause*

I'll put it up here. (*She puts the
remote out of reach*) The remote.
You won't fall on it up here? (*She
gets back into bed*)

Laurence and Lynn enter

Lynn Moved the bathroom? And then he turns the telly on? At three o'clock in the morning? *What* are they called?

Laurence (*shortly*) Kevin and Sharon.

Lynn Very funny pair. You're right.

They get back into bed

Melanie I *told* you not to leave the suitcase there.

Miles Last night the suitcase was *here*. The bathroom was *there* ...

Melanie Aren't you going, then? After all that?

Miles *This* was the suitcase — *that* was the bathroom.

Melanie lies down and turns away from Miles

Lynn I said you're right.

Laurence I heard you.

Lynn I thought you'd be laughing.

Laurence Did you? (*He turns off the side light*)

Miles Turn the light out, then.

Miles exits into the bathroom

The bathroom lights come on

Melanie What, and start all over again?

Miles (*off*) I'm there now. Go back to sleep!

Melanie It's not anything to laugh about, you know. Waking everyone up. Spoiling their holiday. Making a complete fool of yourself.

Lynn turns on the light

Lynn Go on, then.
Laurence What?
Lynn What have I done wrong?
Laurence What do you mean?
Lynn I've done something wrong.
    I've said the wrong thing.
Laurence Let's get some sleep.
    (*He turns the light out*)

Lynn turns the light on

Lynn What was it?
Laurence Forget it. (*He turns the
    light out*)

Lynn turns the light on

Lynn What, the car? Because I
    said about the car?
Laurence *Someone's* got to think
    about the car!
Lynn Fine, good, think about the
    car, nobody's stopping you!
Laurence You don't have to go
    shouting it out to everyone in the
    world! (*He turns the light out*)

The bathroom Lights go off

Miles enters from the bathroom

Miles I said turn out the light. If you
    want to go to sleep.
Melanie (*sitting up in bed*) I feel
    very embarrassed.
Miles *You* feel embarrassed?
Melanie You're always doing this
    kind of thing.
Miles I have never before mistaken
    the position of a hotel bathroom.
Melanie You've fallen over your
    suitcase.
Miles But never on to the remote
    control of a television set.

Melanie You're always —
shouting , and making jokes —
and crashing about ... !
Miles Sh!
Melanie Are *you* shushing *me*?

*Miles gestures at Melanie to keep
her voice down*

You think they've got back to
sleep after all that? I'll tell you
what they're doing. They're
talking about us.

Lynn turns her light on

Lynn What, you think they're lying
there talking about you?
Laurence I don't care what they're
doing.

Miles I might have expected a bit
of sympathy, a bit of loyalty. I
could have broken my leg.

I just don't like you shooting
your mouth off about me to all
and sundry.

I do in fact have a rather painful
bruise on my elbow. Never mind,
though. Sleep well

*He lies down and turns his back on
Melanie*

*He lies down and turns his back on
Lynn*

Melanie I wonder if *he* treats *her*
like this? (*She turns out her light*)

Lynn I wonder if *he* treats *her* like
this? (*She turns out her light*)

Darkness. A phrase of music

Darkness. A phrase of music

*Then grey light, followed by pink
light: dawn*

*Then grey light, followed by pink
light: dawn*

(*Sitting up; alarmed*) What time is
it? (*She finds her watch*)

Miles sits up

Miles (*alarmed*) Where are we?

Lynn (*looking at her watch*) Are
we ahead or are we behind?

Melanie (*waking*) What? What is
it?
Miles I can't remember which
country we're in!
Melanie Don't start.
Miles Oh yes. It's "The Place with
the Trouser-press." (*He gets up,
and orientates himself*) Trouser-
press — suitcase — car-park ...

Miles looks round carefully

*Laurence gets up and heads straight
for the window*

Lynn What, the car?
Laurence What?
Lynn You're going to look at the
car?
Laurence I'm on my way to the
bathroom. (*He diverts sharply to
the bathroom*) All right?

Laurence exits into the bathroom

Bathroom! All right?
Melanie I said, don't start.

Miles exits into the bathroom

The bathroom lights come on

Melanie gets up

Lynn gets up

Lynn (*concessively*) Don't worry.
I'll have a look..

Melanie What sort of day is it?

Melanie goes out on to the balcony   Lynn goes out on to the balcony

Melanie Oh. Sorry!
Lynn Sorry!

Melanie goes back inside again

Lynn gazes down at the car park

Melanie goes out on to the balcony again

Melanie Sorry about all the performance in the night.
Lynn Oh, no. We just didn't know what was happening. He thought it was the revolution breaking out.
Melanie I was so embarrassed.
Lynn No, mine's just as bad. Night before last, middle of the night, he gets up, and yes, he finds the bathroom, no problem, but then what happens? I don't know ... he won't turn the light on; he starts crashing about; I say "For heaven's sake turn the light on!" — he *won't* turn the light on ... Next thing I know everything's going smash, crash ... I go running in; the floor's covered in broken glass, and he starts shouting at *me* — somehow it's all my fault!

Lynn peers down at the car park

Melanie What — your car?
Lynn See if it's all right. I got into hot water over that, too. Shouldn't have said he was worried about it. He was *furious!*
Melanie *He* was furious! I don't know what *he'd* got to be furious about. I *told* him not to leave his suitcase there!
Lynn Wouldn't speak, mine!
Melanie I quite like it when they won't speak.

Lynn peers down

  (*Looking down as well*) Which one is it?
Lynn I can't remember.
Melanie What colour is it?
Lynn I've forgotten. What colour's yours?
Melanie Search me.
Lynn I don't know what we're doing here, tell you the truth.
Melanie *I* don't know what we're doing here!
Lynn I don't know where we're going!

Melanie *I* don't know where we're going!
Lynn *He* dreamed all this up!
Melanie Supposed to be a break for me.
Lynn I'd rather put my feet up with a good book.
Melanie I just want to get on with my work.
Lynn I suppose *they* like it.
Melanie Do they?
Lynn Don't they?
Melanie Not much evidence of it.
Lynn He gets in such a state about it.
Melanie He never wants to *meet* anyone.
Lynn Never wants to *meet* anyone!

Both bathroom lights go off

*Laurence and Miles come out of their respective bathrooms and watch
Lynn and Melanie*

Lynn and Melanie realize they are being watched

Melanie Oh, here he is.
Lynn He's giving me a very funny look.
Melanie He'll think we're talking about him.
Lynn They always think you're talking about them!
Melanie See you in breakfast, perhaps.

Lynn and Melanie go back inside

Miles So how's Sharon this
morning?
Melanie Fine.
Miles Telling you all about Kevin?
Melanie Have you finished in the
bathroom?

Laurence So how's the car?
Lynn The car?
Laurence I thought you were look-
ing at the car?
Lynn The car's fine.

Miles Or were you telling her all
about me?
Melanie What colour's our car?
Miles They haven't broken into it?

Melanie I said what colour is it?
Miles They haven't *taken* it?

Miles goes out on to the balcony   *Laurence goes out on to the balcony*

                                             Lynn Don't you believe me?
                                             Laurence See what sort of day it
                                                is ...

During the following Lynn and Melanie pack their bags

Laurence Oh — hallo!
Miles Sorry — just checking the car's still there.
Laurence OK?
Miles Seems to be. Yours all right?
Laurence Hadn't thought. Let's have a look. Yes, still there. Still got four
   wheels.
Miles Sorry about ... You know ... In the night.
Laurence No, I sympathize. Diabolical, the way they move the bathrooms
   around in these places. You'd think they'd standardize. You'd think
   Brussels would do something.
Miles Have the same layout everywhere.
Laurence By law.
Miles TV here, bathroom there.
Laurence You find the bathroom — you *still* don't know where you are. One
   night you've got the basin here, you've got the loo there. Next night — the
   basin's here, the loo's there.
Miles You get up in the middle of the night ...
Laurence Night before last. Don't want to disturb *her* ——
Miles — so you don't turn the light on ——
Laurence Don't turn the light on. And there I am in the bathroom bending
   down ——
Miles — feeling for the loo ——
Laurence — feeling for the loo ——
Miles — which in fact is behind you ——
Laurence — which in fact is behind me ——
Miles — so your head ——
Laurence — unknown to me ——
Miles — is in the basin.
Laurence Suddenly ——
Miles Thump!
Miles Hot tap — *here*. Jump up. Hit the back of my head against the shelf
   over the basin.

Miles Crack!
Laurence Glass shelf.
Miles Of course.
Laurence Not fixed.
Miles Certainly not.
Laurence Loose on its brackets.
Miles Naturally.
Laurence Plus various glass tumblers, pots of face cream et cetera, make-up et cetera et cetera.
Miles Glass everywhere.
Laurence All over the floor.
Miles Bare feet.
Laurence In the dark.
Miles Your wife comes running.
Laurence "What are you playing at?"
Miles "You'll wake the whole hotel!"
Laurence "Don't come in! Don't move! Just turn the light on!"
Miles "Where's the light?"
Laurence "Can't find the light!"
Miles Total panic.
Laurence They should standardize the light switches.
Miles Put your hand out, no matter where you are.
Laurence Spain, France, Luxembourg.
Miles On comes the light.
Laurence I mean, it wasn't my idea in the first place.
Miles Going on holiday?
Laurence I'd just as soon do the garden, quite frankly.
Miles I shouldn't mind working, to tell you the truth. I quite like working.
Laurence But you put yourself out.
Miles Whatever you do you know it's not going to be right.
Laurence Ah well.
Miles There you go.
Laurence What would we do without them?
Miles Holidays?
Laurence No ... (*He nods in the direction of the room*)

Lynn and Melanie, packing, watch Laurence and Miles curiously

Miles Oh. Yes. Right. What indeed?
Laurence Bless their hearts.
Miles Anyway, you got back to sleep in the end?
Laurence Out like a light. You and Sharon?
Miles Me and ...?

Laurence Sharon? Got a bit of sleep?
Miles Oh — us — yes. Fine, fine.
Laurence Well, better go and shave.
Miles On into the great unknown.
Laurence Wonder where the bathroom'll be tonight?
Miles Touch of mystery to our lives.
Laurence See you in breakfast?
Miles Yes, you must meet Sharon.
Laurence Been nice talking to you, Kevin.

Miles and Laurence go back into their rooms

Melanie (*coolly*) I'm glad you've
found someone to talk to at last.
Miles Me and Kevin? We're like
that together.

> **Lynn** (*coolly*) Well, you seem to
> have found a soul-mate.
> **Laurence** What, old Kevin? He's
> all right.

We're having breakfast with
them.

> Thought we might all meet up
> over breakfast.
> **Lynn** Oh, well, this is a change.

> *Lynn exits into the bathroom*

> *The bathroom light comes on*

"We've all done it, Kevin. We've
all been there. We've all had
troubles with the bathroom.
Women, Kevin? They're all
alike."
Melanie (*shocked*) You didn't call
him Kevin?
Miles I didn't call him Kevin. *He*
called *me* Kevin.
Melanie *He* called *you* Kevin?
Miles "You and Sharon get back to
sleep all right, Kevin?" You're
Sharon.

Melanie He called me Sharon?

Miles He wants to meet you properly over breakfast. Two Kevins — two Sharons — we're going to get on like a house on fire.

Melanie gazes at Miles in horror

The bathroom light goes off

Lynn enters from the bathroom, holding toilet stuff to pack

Lynn Well, just as long as you don't go calling him Kevin.

Laurence What do you want me to call him? Nigel?

Lynn You didn't ...

Laurence Didn't what?

Lynn Call him Kevin just now? You didn't call him Kevin out there?

Laurence Kevin, yes. Why not? Kevin. What's wrong?

Melanie He heard you! Everything you said about them! He heard you!

Lynn gazes at Laurence in horror

Lynn He *told* you he's called Kevin?

Laurence I *know* he's called Kevin!

Lynn Because you were listening through the wall, you turnip!

Come on — finish packing! Let's get out of here!

Miles Breakfast ...

Melanie I couldn't look them in the eye!

Miles Come on — be reasonable.

Melanie I *am* being reasonable!

Miles We'll make a joke of it.

Melanie *They've* made the joke of it already. Somebody else making the jokes for once. Close your case up.

Melanie hurls together the last of the packing	*Lynn hurls together the last of the packing*
	We'll get breakfast on the road somewhere.
	Laurence We've paid for breakfast here.
	Lynn What, and sit there with Kevin and Sharon, and them knowing we've had our ear to the wall?
Quick, before we meet them in the corridor!	
	Come on, or we'll be meeting them in the corridor!
That the lot?	
	Have we got everything?
Come on.	
Miles and Melanie open the door, and struggle out with their luggage	*Lynn and Laurence open the door and struggle out with their luggage*
	Lynn Buck up, buck up!
Oh, hallo!	
	Hallo!
Miles Thought we'd give breakfast a miss, after all.	
	Laurence Us, too.
Hit the road.	
	Beat the traffic.
Melanie (*off*) Hold on. Just check we've got everything ...	

*They enter, Melanie pushing
Miles back into the room. She
closes the door behind them*

Miles What?

*They enter, Lynn pushing
Laurence back into the room.
She closes the door behind them*

Laurence What?
Lynn Let them get out of the way
first.

Melanie Give them a head start.
Miles I don't know why *they're*
going.
Melanie (*grimly*) Don't you?

Laurence I don't know why *they're*
going.
Lynn (*grimly*) Don't you?

They wait

They wait. Lynn listens at the door

Laurence (*looking round the room*)
Bit of our life.
Lynn What?
Laurence I said it's a bit of our life.
This room.
Lynn I know.

Miles (*looking round the room*)
And so another chapter in the
story closes behind us.

Laurence Haven't left anything?

No sign we were ever here.
Melanie The lampshade wasn't
that shape when we arrived ...

Lynn Bit of my lifeblood up there
on the ceiling ...

They wait

They wait

Miles They must have gone by
now.

Actually, if they've gone ...

We could have breakfast.
Melanie Don't be silly.

Miles Leave now, we'll bump into
them in the car-park.

Pause. Melanie puts her case down

Melanie Quickly, then ...
Miles Breakfast?

*Melanie flings the door open.
They exit, then return, Melanie
bundling Miles back inside again*

Melanie Why do I ever listen to
anything you say?

*Melanie picks up the bags and leads
Miles on to the balcony*

Fire escape!
Miles Fire escape?

What fire escape?

Laurence Listen ... Silence.

If they've gone ...

We could have breakfast.

Lynn I just want to get out of here.

Laurence They'll still be paying
their bill.

Pause. Lynn puts her case down

Lynn Breakfast.

*Lynn flings the door open. They
exit, then return, Lynn bundling
Laurence back inside again*

I knew it, I knew it!

*Lynn picks up the bags and leads
Laurence on to the balcony*

Balcony!
Laurence Balcony?

We're five floors up!

Melanie (*merrily*) Oh, hallo!

Lynn (*merrily*) Hallo!

Quicker. Possibly. We thought.

Yes! Only ... *bump*!

Yes!

So ...

Melanie laughs merrily and goes back inside

Lynn laughs merrily and goes back inside

Miles makes a helpless gesture to Laurence, and follows Melanie back in. Melanie dumps the luggage and sits down on the edge of the bed

Laurence makes a helpless gesture to Miles, and follows Lynn back in. Lynn dumps the luggage and sits down on the edge of the bed

Miles Now what?
Melanie Stay.
Miles Stay?
Melanie Until we see them get in their car.
Miles We might be here all night! (*He sits down beside her on the bed*)
Melanie We might be here forever.
Miles ⎱ (*together, in despair*)
Melanie ⎰ Doomed to be doubles!

Laurence Now what?
Lynn Stay.
Laurence Stay?
Lynn Until we see them get in their car.
Laurence We might be here all night! (*He sits down beside Lynn on the bed*)
Lynn We might be here forever.
Laurence ⎱ (*together, in despair*)
Lynn ⎰ Doomed to be doubles!

CURTAIN

ACT II

LEAVINGS

The same set as Alarms

When the play begins, John, Jocasta, Nicholas, and Nancy are sitting round the table with empty wine glasses before them. Nancy's arm is in a sling. John is asleep

Pause

Nicholas Well ...
Nancy Well ...

Pause

Jocasta Shall I make some more coffee?
Nicholas No, we really ought to be ——
Nancy (*looking at her watch*) Oh my God, yes — look at the time!
Nicholas (*looking at his watch*) How did it get to be so late?

Pause

Nancy We were going to be going half an hour ago.
Nicholas Yes — how come we're still sitting here?

Pause

Nancy Well, then ...
Nicholas (*looking at John*) We must let these good people get some sleep.
Jocasta (*to John*) Darling ...
Nicholas Don't wake him.
Nancy Busy day.
Nicholas Privilege of the host.
Nancy We'll just quietly slip away.

Pause

Jocasta You don't have to go dashing off.
Nicholas Some of us have got to get up in the morning.

Pause

Jocasta Well, if you've really got to ...
Nicholas Come on, then.
Nancy Lovely evening.

Nicholas and Nancy push their chairs back.

Jocasta (*nudging John; firmly*) Darling ... They're leaving ...
John (*waking up*) Yes, we've got to be going. (*He looks at his watch*) Oh my
  God, look at the time!
Jocasta Darling!
John How did it get to be so late? Some of us have got to get up in the
  morning! Come on, then. (*He gets to his feet*) Lovely evening. We must let
  these good people get some sleep ... (*He stops, confused*)
Jocasta Honestly!
Nicholas Well, if you've really got to ...
John No, no ...
Nicholas We mustn't stop you.
Jocasta You live here. Remember?
John No, no, no, no ...
Jocasta What do you mean, no, no, no, no?
Nancy Don't worry! We can take a hint!

Nicholas and Nancy get to their feet

John I mean, *you* sit down! Go on — sit down, sit down, sit down, sit down!
  Have another glass of wine! (*He refills their glasses*)
Jocasta They were just going!
John Nonsense! Sit down!
Nicholas It's taken us an hour to get on our feet.
John Sit down!
Nicholas You slept through the entire negotiations!
John I wasn't asleep!
Nicholas He wasn't asleep.
John I was thinking.
Nicholas Deep in thought.
John About what you were saying. Sit down!
Nicholas What *were* we saying?
Nancy We weren't saying anything.

Nicholas Long silences.
Nancy While we were waiting for *you* to speak.
John About machines.
Nicholas About machines?
John About burglar alarms and answering machines.
Nicholas Oh, that!
Nancy Then!
Jocasta That was when we got back from Casualty!
Nancy Was that this evening?
Nicholas Good God, have you been asleep since then?
John What you were saying ...
Nancy Bye bye. (*She kisses John*) Thank you so much. I'm sorry about the
    ... (*She indicates her arm*)
Jocasta No — all our fault.
Nancy Don't come out.

Nancy exits L, followed by Jocasta

John What you were saying ——
Nicholas Listen, we'll continue this another time.
John — was that there was something unnatural about our dependence on
    all these machines.
Nicholas Very enjoyable evening. Though actually that isn't what I was
    saying.
John Oh, I thought it was.
Nicholas We can't start all this again now, but as a matter of fact *you* were
    saying it was unnatural.
John *You* were saying it was unnatural, and I was saying, no, what would
    be unnatural, now that these machines have been invented, now that
    they're actually in existence, would be *not* to use them.
Nicholas No, what I was saying, what I was trying to say, was that it was very
    natural to use them ——
John "Unnatural' was the word you actually employed.
Nicholas No, what I actually said was that it was only *too* natural ——
John Only too natural — exactly.
Nicholas Only too natural doesn't mean unnatural.
John Of course it does. Only too natural means *unnaturally* natural.
Nicholas Unnaturally natural? This is an interesting concept ... (*He sits
    down*)
John What's odd about something being unnaturally natural?
Nicholas What's odd about something being unnaturally natural? Look ...
    Sit down, sit down.

John sits

Supposing I said something was naturally unnatural.

Nancy enters L

John You might well say that.
Nancy Oh no!
John Something might well be naturally unnatural.
Nancy You haven't sat down again?
Nicholas Give me an example of something naturally unnatural.

Jocasta enters L

John This table is naturally unnatural.
Jocasta They've sat down again!
John This glass is naturally unnatural.
Nancy I thought we were going?
John This chair is naturally unnatural.
Nancy Come on!
Nicholas You mean it's unnatural by nature?
John I mean it's unnatural by nature.
Nicholas Like an answering machine or a burglar alarm?

Nancy sits down in exasperation

Don't start sitting down again! (*To John*) Like an answering machine or a burglar alarm? (*To Nancy*) I thought we were going?

Nancy gets up

(*To Nancy*) I thought you were arguing that they were natural?

Nancy forces Nicholas up and propels him towards the door. John follows

John Yes! Naturally natural!
Nicholas But now you're saying they're naturally unnatural!
John No, I'm not — I'm saying they're not unnaturally natural! No — not unnaturally unnatural ... No, hold on ...
Nicholas I don't know what we're talking about.
John *I* don't know what we're talking about.

Nicholas and John exit L

Nancy (*turning back to Jocasta*) Sorry. First they won't say anything ...

Jocasta Then they won't stop.
Nancy I know — I meant to ask you about Ariadne ...

Nancy exits L

Jocasta, following Nancy, stops

Jocasta You haven't heard?

Nancy enters L

Nancy Heard what?
Jocasta About Ariadne!
Nancy No?
Jocasta She's left Reggie.
Nancy Left Reggie? Ariadne has left Reggie?
Jocasta According to Joanna.
Nancy What — somebody else?
Jocasta You'll never guess! Grantley Forward!
Nancy Grantley Forward? Reggie — and Grantley Forward?
Jocasta Ariadne and Grantley Forward!
Nancy No!
Jocasta Yes!
Nancy But I thought Grantley ——
Jocasta With Georgina, yes. But you know that Georgina ——
Nancy And Luciano ——
Jocasta For years!
Nancy For years!
Jocasta Well, apparently he came back unexpectedly one day ——

Nicholas enters L, *and waits with ostentatious impatience*

Nancy Luciano?
Jocasta Grantley! And found the two of them manacled to the bed together!
Nancy Luciano and Georgina?
Jocasta No!
Nicholas John's standing on the pavement out there. They'll arrest him for loitering.
Nancy Georgina and *Reggie*?
Nancy Amanda and Laurence!
Nancy Amanda and Laurence? Who are they?
Jocasta No-one knows!

Nicholas takes Nancy by the arm

Nicholas It's like getting the couple in the weather house outdoors at the same time.

Nicholas kisses Jocasta

Nancy Amanda and Laurence?
Nicholas No, no! Good-night. Thank you so much. Loved the bit in Casualty.

Nicholas and Nancy exit L

Nancy (*off*) But I don't understand ...
Jocasta (*calling*) I'll give you a ring in the morning. 'Night 'night! Love to Charlie and Georgie!

Jocasta yawns

Nicholas enters L

Jocasta stops yawning

Nicholas You know Charlie got 98% in maths?
Jocasta Yes, Nancy said!
Nicholas He was so cross about it, though! He said, "Dad, I got one wrong." And when he showed me the paper ——
Jocasta It was the teacher who'd got it wrong!
Nicholas Sorry, sorry.
Jocasta No, no — nice to hear it confirmed. 'Night 'night.

Nicholas exits L *and returns, guiltily*

Nicholas And Theodora? I meant to ask earlier.
Jocasta She's doing very well.
Nicholas The remedial reading ...?
Jocasta Is really helping. We're terribly pleased.

John enters L

John Have you two separated?
Nicholas Sorry. I was just asking about Theodora.
John What, this remedial caper?
Nicholas I gather it's really doing the trick.
John Yes — she can read quite long words now.
Nicholas Marvellous!

John Like the "Play" on the video.
Jocasta She can read *all* the video controls.
John Except "Stop". She can't read "Stop".
Nicholas Anyway ...
Jocasta What she needs is you to believe in what she's doing.
John What she needs is everyone to stop fussing.

Nancy enters L

Nancy You can see the stars moving out there if you watch for long enough.
Jocasta Sorry. We're talking about Theodora.
Nancy Oh, right.
John I mean, it's ridiculous. Some people are *natural* slow readers.
Nicholas *Naturally* natural slow readers?
John *Naturally* natural slow readers — yes.
Nancy I'll sit down. (*She sits*)
Nicholas Don't sit down! We're going, we're going!
Jocasta (*to Nicholas*) No, but bear me out! It's *not* natural not to be reading at her age! It's highly unnatural!
John It's not natural to read at any age!
Jocasta Oh, for heaven's sake!
John Reading is a highly unnatural activity.
Nicholas A *naturally* unnatural activity?
John A *naturally* unnatural activity.
Jocasta Oh, don't start all that again!
John But it is!
Jocasta Come on!

Jocasta exits L

John In fact it's an *unnaturally* unnatural activity ...

John exits L

Nicholas You're still sitting there!
Nancy I want to be absolutely certain you're outside that door before I get to my feet.
Nicholas You're the one who keeps coming back?
Nancy Come on.
Nicholas It would make more sense ... (*he sits*) ... if I stayed sitting down until *you* were outside that door.

Jocasta enters L. *She gazes at Nicholas and Nancy in astonishment*

Jocasta What?
Nicholas We're waiting.
Jocasta Waiting? What for?
Nancy Each other.
Nicholas Together. All right?
Nancy All right — together.

Nicholas and Nancy get to their feet, watching each other. Jocasta watches them

Nicholas Go on.
Nancy Together, yes?
Nicholas We can't get through the door together.
Nancy After you, then.
Nicholas After you.
Nancy Go on.
Nicholas No, no.
Jocasta *I'll* go.

Jocasta exits L

Nancy (*to Jocasta*) We're going to end up like those two manacled to the bed.

Nancy exits L

Nicholas What, Laurence Troon and Amanda Wivenhoe?

Nancy enters L

Nancy It was Laurence *Troon*? And Amanda *Wivenhoe*?
Nicholas According to George Worrall.
Nancy You said you didn't know!
Nicholas I didn't say anything.
Nancy But this is terrible!

Nancy pushes the door to

Nicholas What? What's happening?
Nancy Amanda Wivenhoe lives with Charlie's maths tutor!
Nicholas Yes, but he can't really complain. He's also involved with that
  Kung Fu woman in Huddersfield ...
Nancy But if Charlie's maths tutor finds out about Amanda and Laurence
  Troon ... (*she sits down*) ... and moves in with the Kung Fu woman ——

Nicholas In Huddersfield ...?
Nancy — then who do we get to tutor Charlie?
Nicholas Oh, my God! (*He sits down*)
Nancy He doesn't know about Laurence Troon so far?
Nicholas I've no idea.
Nancy Who told you?
Nicholas George Worrall.

Jocasta and John enter L

Nancy Who presumably got it from Patsy.
Nicholas Who will have told Clarissa.
Nancy Who knows the Pillingtons.
Nicholas Who may meet Charlie's maths tutor at the Muldews ...
Nancy We must make absolutely sure it doesn't go any further.
Nicholas I won't tell a soul.
Nancy Not a soul!
Nicholas Not a soul!
John Sorry. We just happened to be outside. Saw the front door was open
  — thought we'd drop in ...
Nancy Yes, sit down, sit down!
Nicholas You're not going to believe this ...
Nancy (*to Nicholas*) Not a *soul*!
Nicholas Not a *soul*!
Nancy It was Laurence Troon and Amanda Wivenhoe!
Jocasta You mean ...?
Nancy Yes!
Jocasta No! (*She sits*)

John watches the others

Nicholas And Amanda Wivenhoe lives with Charlie's maths tutor!
Nancy Who's also involved with this woman in Huddersfield ...
Nicholas Who teaches Kung Fu!
Nancy Who teaches Kung Fu!
Nicholas So what's going to happen?
Nancy He's going to leave Amanda ...
Nicholas And go zooming up to Huddersfield!
John Laurence Troon?
Nancy ⎫
Nicholas ⎬ (*together*) Charlie's maths tutor!
Jocasta ⎭
John (*resignedly*) Oh, Charlie's maths tutor. (*He sits*)
Nancy Another glass of wine?

Nicholas Or something to eat?
Nancy I feel suddenly kind of hollow inside.
John How about breakfast?
Nicholas I'll do it!
Nancy I'll do it!
Nicholas Scrambled eggs?
Nancy A bit of bacon?
Jocasta Well ...
John Actually ...
Nicholas No, no!
Nancy You sit there ——
Nicholas — and make yourselves at home ...!

Nancy and Nicholas exit towards the kitchen

John and Jocasta settle down again at the table

Chink

They look up apprehensively

CURTAIN

LOOK AWAY NOW

Three aircraft seats

When the play begins, reassuring music is playing

The seats are occupied by three passengers, Aptly, Bloss, and Charr. Bloss is sitting in the middle. All three have folded newspapers

The reassuring music suddenly stops

Stewardess's Voice over PA Now will you please ensure that your seat-belt is securely fastened, ready for take-off.

Passengers Aptly and Charr gaze absently and expressionlessly into space. Charr yawns. Passenger Bloss automatically checks his seat-belt, then the seat back and arm rest during the following

Your table should be folded away, with the seat-back upright and the arm-rest down. Your mind should be in the closed position to be adopted when routine safety announcements of this sort are made.

Aptly glances at Bloss, and Bloss stops

If you are still conscious at this time, you may find the level tone of voice in which this announcement is being made helpful in securing complete inattention. In the pocket in front of you will find a card showing aircraft safety procedures.

Bloss automatically moves to look for the card. Aptly glances at him again, and Bloss sits back and gazes into space

In the interest of your own peace of mind, please studiously ignore this. Any attempt to look at it may result in your appearing nervous or inexperienced to your fellow-passengers. We are mentioning it purely as a test to make sure that no-one is listening.

The cabin attendants will now demonstrate the use of the aircraft's emergency oxygen masks and life-jackets.

Aptly and Charr immediately open their newspapers and become absorbed in them.

They are not trained in mime or the use of theatrical properties, and they find this performance profoundly embarrassing. It is important to them to know that no-one is watching. Faces should be completely obscured by newspapers, or eyes securely shut.

Seeing Aptly and Charr, Bloss hastily opens his own newspaper

If for any reason the cabin air-supply should fail, oxygen will be provided. Masks like this will appear automatically. We say "like this", but what in fact these masks are like you have of course no idea.

Bloss happens to glance over the top of his paper, and does a double-take. His mouth falls open

In the unlikely event of anyone looking up and finding out, please remain seated. Place the newspaper back in front of your face and try to breathe normally.

Bloss lifts the newspaper in front of his face again

The action of pulling the mask to the face automatically opens the way to less inhibited behaviour. This may be required after a landing on water, when you will find that you have no idea where your life-jacket is stowed.

Bloss peers cautiously round the edge of his newspaper, amazed at the sight that meets his eyes

To prepare for immersion, check that your shirt is free from the waistband of the trousers or skirt, then pull it upwards over the head in one steady movement, like this. It is particularly important that no-one watches any part of what follows.

Bloss hurriedly vanishes again

Release the catch at the waistband, pull down the fastener provided, and let the lower garments fall to the floor. Please ensure that they do not obstruct the emergency exits.

Bloss emerges from his newspaper again, vanishes in horror, then slowly re-emerges as his newspaper sinks, and gazes in covert fascination

There is a whistle attached to your life-jacket for attracting attention, but this is under your seat with the life-jacket, and you may wish to try alternative methods of persuading people to look at you.

Bloss looks at Aptly and Charr to see if they have seen what he has seen, but they are still deep in their newspapers. He gazes open-mouthed at the demonstration

Ladies should undo the fastenings at the front of the upper undergarment as shown, and pass it backwards over the shoulders, like this.

Aptly glances up from his newspaper and sees Bloss watching. He is amused by Bloss's naïvety. Charr glances up as well. Aptly nods discreetly in the direction of Bloss. Charr smiles as well

Now, peel any hosiery downwards, like this, followed by the lower undergarment, taking care to keep the pelvis rotating at the same time, as shown. Once off, the undergarments may, if desired, be passed around various parts of the body, like this, then tossed lightly into the faces of potential rescuers, who may be engrossed in reading matter at least as deeply as passengers are now.

Bloss suddenly realizes he is being watched and hastily snatches up his newspaper. It disintegrates into its various component pages

If necessary, the pressure can be increased by applying the mouth to this mouthpiece, but gentlemen, no pipes or cigars, please. For your own safety and comfort, kindly do not inflame other passengers until you are outside the aircraft.

A faint suspicion that they are missing something has now come to Aptly and Charr

Now please allow cabin staff a few seconds to retrieve their clothes and retire to the galley areas to dress.

Aptly and Charr turn to look at what Bloss was looking at. There is nothing to be seen. They glance in puzzlement at Bloss

Thank you for your complete lack of attention.

Bloss glances at the others, and smiles. He has a little mystery to himself

Cabin staff will shortly be commencing the meal service. Please note, however, that Passenger Bloss, in Seat 31B, who was caught peeping during the safety demonstration, will get no pudding.

Bloss's triumph turns to shame; Aptly and Charr's bafflement into triumph

CURTAIN

HEART TO HEART

A doorway

Beyond the doorway a party is taking place; there emerges a confused and deafening roar of party conversation

When the play begins, Charmian is talking inaudibly to Peter

Clifford enters

Peter moves away and exits

Clifford and Charmian begin to talk, in the most natural and friendly manner, but we can't hear a word they say

Clifford [I don't think we've met. My name's Clifford.]
Charmian [What?]

The background noise fades during the following so we hear what they are saying

Clifford I don't think we've met. My name's Clifford.
Charmian Oh, so do I!
Clifford Do you think anybody in this room can hear what anyone else is saying?
Charmian I wonder if anyone can hear a word that anyone else is saying.
Clifford I suppose there's one person who can, and that's God. I picture him looking down   ... (*he turns down an imaginary dial*)   ... and tuning everything else out   ...
Charmian (*baffled*) Sorry?
Clifford I said, I picture God looking down ... (*he repeats the gesture*) ... and tuning everything else out. What I imagine. God looking down. Tuning out the noise. *God.*
Charmian *Very* odd, the whole occasion!
Clifford So he can hear what you and I are *saying*!
Charmian *Completely* insane!
Clifford There we are, clear as a *bell*!
Charmian *Such* hell! Why do we do it?

Clifford Both of us smiling and nodding away.

Charmian Away? Yes, we have. To Egypt, which was rather a *lark*!

Clifford Like a drain, I should think, when he realizes we haven't the slightest idea what we're smiling and nodding *about*.

Charmian Oh, a *brief* bout. You mean, of *tummy*?

Clifford Hilarious.

Charmian Well, *mildly* delirious. And *you*? Have *you* managed to get away yet?

Clifford Not a word, no.

Charmian Oh, marvellous!

Clifford Not a single word you've uttered.

Charmian How wonderful!

Clifford Have you heard anything *I've* said?

Charmian No ... No ... I don't think we have. Not *there* exactly. But you'd recommend it, would you?

Clifford I know you're asking me something.

Charmian Of course. Quite. I understand that.

Clifford Is it: do I live round here? Or is it: did I see some ghastly wildlife programme on television?

Charmian Oh, we *love* the wildlife ones! How about you?

Clifford Just up the *road*.

Charmian No, we *missed* the one about the toad! So do you live round here?

Clifford No, I didn't.

Charmian Where are *you*, then?

Clifford Because I *hate* them.

Charmian Oh, the Stopfords live there! Tim and Lise! Do you *know* them?

Clifford Yes! *Loathe* them!

Charmian *Do* you? Tim and Lise?

Clifford Chimpanzees, yes — they're the ones I loathe most.

Charmian *Tremendously* old friends!

Clifford All those disgusting tricks they get up to with *bananas*.

Charmian Mad as hatters! But so *sweet*!

Clifford Eat?

Charmian Oh, I just *adore* them!

Clifford So would I, but there's a frightful *scrum*.

Charmian *Frightful* fun! Such get up and *go*!

Clifford Get up and *what*?

Charmian Go!

Clifford Go?

Charmian Don't you think?

Clifford What — *together*?

Charmian *So* together!

Clifford You mean — *now*?

Charmian I mean — *wow*!
Clifford Right! Yes! Why not? I mean — if you're *free* ...
Charmian Us? No — *two*. Two girls. Terribly hard work, but we do have an *au pair*.
Clifford Go where? *Any*where, provided we can get out of this *noise*.
Charmian Boys? Wonderful!
Clifford Fine!
Charmian *Nine*?
Clifford Absolutely! Except — this is ridiculous ——
Charmian No, very brave of you.
Clifford — I didn't quite catch your *name*.
Charmian *Quite* a game, I should think. I can't imagine how you cope!
Clifford Cope?
Charmian I couldn't *begin* to cope!
Clifford Braginta Cope?
Charmian No! Couldn't *possibly* cope!
Clifford Sorry — *Cosima* Cope. Yes? Cosima Cope?
Charmian Oh, I see. Because of the *Pope*?
Clifford Cosima *Pope*, right. Got there. Cosima *Pope*.
Charmian But you're allowed to use the *rhythm* method, aren't you?
Clifford So do I! We'll find a place where we can dance!

Clifford takes Charmian by the arm and leads her towards the exit

Well, I don't think *we* gave God any cause for amusement, did we? I think He'd have been rather *impressed*!
Charmian Yes, come on, *I'd* need a rest if *I* had nine.

Peter enters

Clifford and Charmian come face to face with Peter

Peter (*to Clifford*) Hallo, I don't think we've met.
Clifford Yes, I remember.
Peter I'm Peter.
Clifford You're David.
Peter Peter Spatchworth.
Clifford David, David — don't tell me — isn't it *Hopper*?
Peter Sweltering. And you've met my wife?
Clifford No.
Peter No?
Clifford She's away in Belgium, unfortunately.
Peter Oh, well, let me introduce you.

Clifford Of course. Cosima. Cosima Pope. But we've got to be popping.
Peter Poppin? *You* are?
Clifford Sadly.
Peter (*to Charmian*) Stanley? Darling, this is Stanley Poppin. (*To Clifford*)
  Clifford!
Clifford Isn't she? But I saw her first, so hands *off*!
Peter Yes, we must be off, too.
Clifford Nice to see you, David.
Peter Nice to meet you, Stanley. Take care.
Clifford And if we can't we'll name it after you!

*Clifford takes one of Charmian's arms, Peter the other, to lead her off in
different directions*

The party noise resumes and the conversation becomes inaudible again

Clifford [What?]
Peter [What?]
Clifford [What are you doing?]
Peter [What's happening?]
Charmian [What *is* all this? What's going on?]
Clifford [Do you mind?]

*Clifford takes Peter's hand off Charmian's arm. Clifford pulls Charmian
away from Peter. Peter pushes Clifford aside. They begin to struggle.
Charmian tries to intervene. The two men pull her out of the way in different
directions*

*Over the noise of the party conversation there can just be distinguished the
sound of huge cosmic laughter*

The three of them look upwards as they brawl

CURTAIN

GLASSNOST

A lectern with microphones is set, with two glass Autocue plates in front of it

When the play begins, the stage is in darkness. We can hear the hubbub of an audience

Voice over PA My Lords, Ladies, and Gentlemen ...

The hubbub dies away. The Lights come up on the lectern with microphones

Pray silence for the Right Honourable the Baroness Armament KO GBH RSVP.

Right Honourable the Baroness Armament KO GBH RSVP enters, sincerely and energetically

There is tumultuous applause, off

Armament I want to talk to you today about something of vital importance to all of us here. I want to share with you a vision that I have. And if you have an advance press release of the speech you can tear it up, because here I am departing from my prepared text ...

What is it, this vision that I have? I will tell you. It is a vision of the future. A vision that is constantly before my eyes as I speak. It is the vision ...

She stops. The vision before her eyes is not the one she expected to be seeing

It is the vision reflected in these two glass plates.

She looks from one plate to the other. She feels for a script. There is none. She looks into the wings. She looks at the plates again. She recovers herself and continues

You may not even have noticed them. They are designed to be inconspicuous. But they are an essential part of my Autocue, and the vision that I see in them is a vision of the words that I am just about to utter.

You are surprised. You were expecting me to make a major policy statement on regionalization in the watercress industry. You were perhaps hoping for a few caustic asides on burning topics of the day, such as religious education in army catering schools. You were certainly not expecting me to start explaining the mechanics of my Autocue.

Now let me be absolutely frank. I too am surprised. I too was expecting to be addressing you on the subject of watercress. These words that I see hanging in the air before me are not the words that I expected to see. These words that I am uttering with such sincerity and conviction are not the words that I was expecting to utter. I am as mystified as you are.

How, you wonder, do these words of mine come to appear in these two pieces of glass.

I will tell you quite plainly. They are put there by an underpaid operative concealed in the wings. They are put there by a gentleman called Mervyn Stoop.

She gives a long and thoughtful look into the wings, then returns to her speech

Now, let me say this to you today. I am completely dependent upon that wretched underpaid operative. My future, in every sense, is in Mervyn Stoop's hands. The only words I have to put before you are the words that he puts before me. And if Mervyn Stoop has taken it into his head to replace the speech provided, the speech we rehearsed together so recently ... If he has taken it into his head, at the last minute, during the tea-break after the rehearsal, to replace that speech with a few thoughts of his own ——

She turns and casts a long and murderous look into the wings, then turns back and gazes into the glass. Eventually, through grated teeth:

—— then those thoughts of his own are the thoughts which I in all sincerity now find myself sharing with you.

Another look into the wings. Then she resigns herself, and becomes as sincere and confiding as before

There are certain liberties that we all cherish. If I don't like what I'm saying then I am free, I am perfectly free, to stop saying it ... But until I have said all the words in front of me I will get no more words to say. Mervyn Stoop will see to that. Silence will fall.

Pause. Another look into the wings

And will continue.

Pause

Until I have uttered every single word. And performed every single stage direction.

Pause. Then she surrenders, and waggles her fingers in her ears

What is at issue here is a matter of simple right and wrong. During that fateful rehearsal beforehand I took it into my head to scream abuse at Mervyn Stoop. I went further. I discharged him from my employment. Simply because I was left speechless for a fraction of a second while his attention was distracted by an urgent call on his mobile! Simply because of this, I shouted like a lunatic and gave him a week's notice!

There must surely be — I say this quite openly — there must surely be forever a question over the political judgment of someone who gives their Autocue operator a week's notice just before a major speech.

And the sheer injustice of it! Not once in all the time he has worked for me has he abused the absolute trust I have placed in him. Sometimes, it's true, he has speeded up just a touch to reduce the impact of all the absolute nonsense I have spouted over the years about economic policy. But in general he has been right behind me. Or rather he has been right in front of me, and I have been right behind him.

How destructive, how terribly destructive, any failure of that mutual trust can be! Without it I may find myself beginning to go faster, then faster still, faster and faster, until I am gabbling like a lunatic and gazing at you with a mad unblinking stare and my eyeballs wobbling from side to side like ping-pong balls.

And if he suddenly ——

She waits. She looks into the wings

— stops, and jumps it backwards ... And if he suddenly stops, and jumps it backwards ... then you'll hear the same thing twice over ... then you'll hear the same thing twice over ... But I give you this undertaking: it will be every bit as sincere the second time around.

So here is what I pledge today: to improve job security for workers in the electronic prompter industry. I give you my solemn word — no, I will go further: I give you *his* solemn word — to offer all workers in the industry, from today, retrospectively, guaranteed employment for life; to grant them the freedom to fast-forward through anything they find repugnant to their conscience or alien to their interests; and to give them the parking rights which some of them have been so long denied.

Trust me to lead you through the difficult days that lie ahead. Remember: one step in front of me will always be Mervyn Stoop!

She snatches one of the glass plates off its stand and advances vengefully upon the wings

Curtain

TOASTERS

A table is set with a wine bottle — nearly empty — on it

The Lights come up on Spott, Much, and Candle. They are standing, and have been standing for some time. Each is holding, as best he or she can, a plate, a knife and fork, a napkin, a wine glass, and a folder of papers. The folders are full; the plates are empty. So are the glasses belonging to Spott and Candle

Speaker's Voice (*off*) ... and I believe, moreover, that we can look back with some satisfaction upon a period that was marked by its considerable achievements as well as by its inevitable disappointments, a period that will be remembered as a time of searching and of sometimes finding, of striving and of sometimes prevailing; of progress, yes, but also of consolidation; of expansion but also of retrenchment.

During the following:

Spott discreetly suppresses a yawn

Much discreetly finishes up the last of his wine. Spott and Candle discover that their glasses are empty. Spott spies a bottle with a little wine in it on the other side of Candle. He discreetly draws Candle's attention to it. Candle discreetly contrives to get hold of it, whereupon the others discreetly hold out their glasses to be refilled

Candle is now holding one more object than it is humanly possible to hold. As he pours, the folder of papers slips away from him, to be fielded by Much, who now in his turn has one more object than ... etc.. Much's knife and fork slip away to be fielded by Spott, who now has ... etc..

I must, I think, here sound a note of caution. When we turn from the recent past to the immediate and longer-term future, we are looking at a projected shortfall, as against previous estimates, of something in the order of three to four per cent on the unadjusted figures, *provided*, and I cannot stress this sufficiently, *provided* there is no corresponding fall-away in the overall uplift, which, in real terms, constitutes scarcely more than standstill funding at a time when the underlying upward trend has been more than offset by a combination of declining returns and returning declines. Suffice it to say that we shall be monitoring results in this area very carefully, and that swift corrective measures will be implemented if need be to keep short-term fluctuations within the parameters established before the present downturn in ongoing upswing. But, that being said, perhaps we should try to end on a more positive note. If you would turn for one moment to the papers you have in your folder ——

Pause. Aghast at this unexpected demand, they attempt to juggle their folders open

—you will see that the figures there have a significant and not unencouraging story to tell. It is all the more gratifying, I think, in view of the prevailing climate of uncertainty, to find, turning for a moment to page 3 ... page 3 ——

They struggle to turn to page 3; during the following they try to follow the Speaker's instructions

— that underlying performance for the current period has been so relatively unaffected, if due allowance is made for changes in the way in which data are recorded, changes that are fully explained in the notes at the bottom of page 29 ... Some further allowance must also be made for the inevitable unforeseen factors, if you would turn for a moment to page 37 ... Does everyone have page 37 ...? You will note in the righthand column a further adjustment for certain non-recurring eventualities such as changes in cut-off levels, to be found in the table on page 15 ... And on page 22 in the *pink* pages — the *pink* pages — a once-only provision for assets written off or written down since the previous valuation. In fact the year-on-year figures, turning back to page 3 — and I commend them to your particular attention ... This is page 3 — page 3 — in the *white* pages ... On page 51 of which, incidentally, you will find a most important date, and I would ask you to make a note of it in your diaries *now* ... Thank you. Turning once again to page 3 — you will see that the all-important global interim figures show a slight but perceptible rise in percentage terms, and in the current climate that is a result on which I think all concerned must be congratulated ...

Pause. There is the sound of uncertain applause

Spott, Much, and Candle struggle to join in with the applause, tucking glasses under arms, or putting them down on the floor

Now you will all make sure your glasses are charged ...

They snatch up their glasses and discover first that they are empty, then that the bottle is empty as well

I want to propose a toast to the person who more than anyone else made this remarkable achievement possible. You can probably guess who I'm referring to when I say that this person is a member of a team all of whom have consistently achieved above-average results in office economy, and one of whom, Richard Food, has succeeded in being named twice running as runner-up in the monthly organizational motivation competition ——

They raise their glasses, concealing their emptiness

— which I think in itself deserves a round of applause.

Applause

Spott, Much, and Candle hurriedly struggle to put their glasses down, or on the floor, in order to join in

So would you please raise your glasses ——

They make haste to recover their glasses and raise them

— and drink a toast to someone who has already enabled this organization to win a regional efficiency award ——

Pause. There is uncertain applause

Spott, Much, and Candle hurriedly struggle to free their hands again

— a particularly splendid piece of news ——

They pick up their glasses

— because it led to our going forward to the national semi-finals ——

Pause. They bend, put their glasses down and raise their hands to applaud

Jane Dumble!

They hastily snatch their glasses up again

Everyone Jane Dumble!

They drink the toast

Applause

They put their glasses down to join in

Speaker's Voice Also Jane Dumble's loyal assistant, James Trodden!

They pick their glasses up

Everyone James Trodden!

Applause

They put their glasses down and join in

Speaker's Voice And while we're drinking toasts I'd like to propose one to Jane's mother, whose 57th birthday falls I gather exactly one week from today.

They pick their glasses up

But I know that first Jane and her mother would wish me to mention the rehabilitation centre that has made this anniversary possible ...

Applause

They put their glasses down

But that having been said ——

They pick their glasses up.

—— we should spare a thought for rehabilitation centres of every sort that do such magnificent work up and down the country ——

Applause

They put their glasses down

Jane's mother!

They pick their glasses up

Much (*on his own*) Jane's mother!

They drink the toast, then bend to put their glasses down

Speaker's Voice Which brings me by the most natural progression to someone else whose birthday falls this month — Lord Overdrive himself.

They stop, half-way down, hesitating between glasses down and glasses up

Lord Overdrive's achievements and services have been so many and so various that I have to ask myself where to begin. Should we rather drink to his health ...? Or applaud his success ...? Raise our glasses to the continuation of his success in the future ...? Or show him our appreciation in the usual way ...? Perhaps it would be most appropriate for us simply to say ——

Pause. They hover between air and earth

Well done!

Spott applauds. Much and Candle drink a toast

Much ⎱
Candle ⎰ (*together, mumbling*) Well done!

Spott, seeing Much and Candle drink the toast, hastily snatches up his glass and drinks the toast as well — just as Much and Candle, seeing Spott applaud, hastily put their glasses down and applaud

Speaker Let us pray ——

Spott drops to her knees

— that we go forward together henceforth ——

Much, seeing Spott, drops to his knees as well, just as Candle hauls Spott to her feet again ...

— to achieve further no less encouraging results. One final point: I realize what a burden has fallen on everyone here today. I know how full everyone's hands have been. So let's end by giving a very special tribute to ourselves. Let's show the world just what we can do, by raising our glasses ——

They raise their glasses

— and clapping *at the same time.*

They applaud at the same time

There is a huge sound of chinking and smashing glass

Everything finally slips away from Much, Spott, and Candle, and goes everywhere. They suck glass out of fingers, put napkins to severed wrists, etc..

CURTAIN

IMMOBILES

There are twelve telephones on stage. Phone A is a domestic phone with an answering machine, c. Phone B is a coin-box in an airport location, L. Phone C is another coin-box in another airport location, R. Phone D is yet another airport location. Phone E is a coin-box in a public house. Phone F is a coin-box at an Underground station. Phone G is a call-box in a railway station. Phone H is a coin-box in a fast-food outlet. Phone I is a coin-box in the street. Phone J is a coin-box in a hospital. Phone K is a coin-box inside a police station. Phone L is a second phone in the public house, right next to phone E

When the play begins, the stage is in darkness. We hear the ringing of a phone

The Lights come up on phone A. The ringing ceases and the answering machine answers

Chris's Voice *Hi! Chris and Nikki aren't here right now, so why don't you wait for the funny little noise, then leave them a funny little message?*

There is a beep

The Lights come up on Dietrich, L. He is standing by a coin-box in an airport location (phone B) holding the receiver, a suitcase at his feet

The Lights go down on the answering machine

Dietrich (*into the phone*) Hallo, yes — Chris and Nikki! It's me, Dietrich. I am so looking forward to seeing you both again! It is so kind of you to come and meet me at the airport — most unnecessary, but a very nice welcome, so thank you — and, well, here I am! At the airport! So, I look forward to seeing you ... I gave you the right date, yes, the 15th? And the time, 18.40 ...? So, no hurry — I wait for you here ... I like very much your humorous message, by the way.

The Lights cross-fade from Dietrich to Chris who is standing by another coin-box R in another airport location (phone C), holding the receiver. He waits, listening

We hear the ringing tone: brr brr, brr brr

Chris's Voice *Hi! Chris and Nikki aren't here right now, so why don't you wait for the funny little noise, then leave them a funny little message?*

Beep

Chris (*into the phone*) Oh, God, that message is a mistake — I must change it ... It's me, Chris, I'm at the airport. No sign of Dietrich, though. There *wasn't* a flight from Düsseldorf at 18.40 ... I just wondered if he'd rung or anything ... Only you're not there for some reason ... Where are you ...? No Dietrich, no, you, just me, standing at Arrivals in Terminal One ... You did say Terminal One ...? I hope this is not the start of one of those terrible sagas ... There's a flight at 19.20, at Terminal *Two*. I'd better go and have a look at that. If he rings, tell him I'll be at Terminal Two. *Two*, yes ...?

The Lights cross-fade from Chris to Dietrich at phone B. He waits, receiver to ear, as before

We hear the ringing tone: brr brr, brr brr

Chris's Voice *Hi! Chris and Nikki aren't here right now, so why don't you wait for the funny little noise, then leave them a funny little message?*

Beep

Dietrich (*into the phone*) Hallo, Chris and Nikki! It's Dietrich again. I like your humorous message even more the second time I hear it ... I'm sorry to be such a pest, but I don't know should I wait here at the airport or not ... I can easily come to your house ... Only, if you are on your way ... Bad traffic, perhaps ... So kind of you ... I will wait here one more hour maybe, and then ... I don't know ... I look forward to see you.

The Lights cross-fade from Dietrich to Nikki at the answering machine (phone A), listening

Dietrich's Voice *... Bad traffic, perhaps ... So kind of you ... I will wait here one more hour maybe, and then ... I don't know ... I look forward to see you.*

There is a long beep

Nikki presses "Record" on the answering machine

Nikki (*into the answering machine*) Hallo, Dietrich, this is a message for Dietrich, from Nikki, in case you ring again. Dietrich, Chris is there, at the airport; there's a message from him on the machine — he missed you somehow, and now he's gone to Terminal Two. Two, OK? I've got to go out again — shop for supper. Sorry to talk so fast, but you have to fit the outgoing message into ——

Beep

— the space, and it's run out already. (*She presses "Record" again*)

The Lights cross-fade from Nikki to Dietrich at phone B

Nikki's Voice ... *and now he's gone to Terminal Two. Two, OK? I've got to go out again — shop for supper. Sorry to talk so fast, but you have to fit the outgoing message into* ——

Beep

Dietrich (*into the phone*) Hallo, Nikki, it's Dietrich again. Well, so — we make contact at last! I heard your message, yes, very good, very clear, thank you, I like it even more than your humorous message. So kind of you. And yes, I will go to Terminal Two. If Chris rings again, tell him to wait there, at Terminal Two. So kind of him to meet me. So sorry to be such a pain in the behind.

The Lights cross-fade from Dietrich to Chris at phone C. He listens patiently

Nikki's Voice ... *and now he's gone to Terminal Two. Two, OK? I've got to go out again — shop for supper. Sorry to talk so fast, but you have to fit the outgoing message into* ...

Beep

Chris (*into the phone*) Yes, well, it's not Dietrich, it's me. So — Dietrich is floating around Heathrow somewhere? Where exactly, of course, you don't bother to say. Not at Terminal *Two*, evidently, because I was *at* Terminal Two. Now I'm back at Terminal *One*. But if he gets your message then he *will* go to Terminal Two ... All right, I'll go to Terminal Two again ... I sometimes seriously wonder if life is worth living ... And where are *you*? I thought your mother was coming today, I thought you were waiting in for your mother — I thought that was why I was meeting Dietrich ...? Right — Terminal Two. If he rings again tell him to stay at Terminal Two ... Maddening — he's your chum, not mine ...

The Lights cross-fade from Chris to Dietrich at phone B

Chris moves to phone D

Nikki's Voice *... and now he's gone to Terminal Two. Two, OK? I've got to go out again — shop for supper. Sorry to talk so fast, but you have to fit the outgoing message into* ——

Beep

Dietrich (*into the phone*) Hallo, Nikki, this is Dietrich. Now things go from bad to worse — I cannot find Terminal Two! There is no Terminal Two at Gatwick! Nikki, do you mean the North Terminal ...? Maybe you mean the North Terminal ... I think I go to the North Terminal ... So kind of you to take all this trouble ...

The Lights cross-fade from Dietrich to Chris, at a third airport location (phone D). He listens to the phone with his eyes closed

Nikki's Voice *... and now he's gone to Terminal Two. Two, OK? I've got to go out again — shop for supper. Sorry to talk so fast, but you have to fit the outgoing message into* ...

Chris (*into the phone*) If I have to listen to that message once more I'll scream — it's even more maddening than the last one ... I'm at Terminal Two, and of course there's no sign of the bloody man ... He might be anywhere! Terminal Three, Terminal Four, the bar, the restaurant, the lavatory ... Unless you said *Gatwick*. You didn't say Gatwick, did you, by any chance ...? You said *don't* go somewhere, I remember that ... Did you say don't go to Gatwick? Or don't go to Heathrow? *Asinine* thing to say — *don't* go somewhere ...

The Lights cross-fade from Chris, still speaking, to Nikki at the answering machine (phone A). She tries to control her irritation

Chris's Voice *... Did you say don't go to Gatwick? Or don't go to Heathrow? Asinine thing to say — don't go somewhere ... But since you're still floating around God knows where there's no way of finding out ... I can't drive to Gatwick now ... I suppose he may have gone back to Terminal One ... I'll try Terminal One again, for the last time, because then I'm coming home ...*

A long beep

Nikki presses "Record"

Nikki (*into the answering machine*) Dietrich, so sorry, my idiot husband has gone to Heathrow, I told him Gatwick, and he went to Heathrow ... ! Don't you listen to a single word I say? Not Dietrich — you! Dietrich, get on the train, there's a train, it goes to Victoria, come to Victoria, I'll jump in the car and meet you at Victoria. Victoria Station. So sorry — we're both longing to ——

Beep

— see you, only now I'm talking to myself again! (*She punches "Record"*)

The Lights cross-fade from Nikki to Dietrich at phone B

Nikki exits C

Nikki's Voice ...*Victoria, I'll jump in the car and meet you at Victoria. Victoria Station. So sorry — we're both longing to ——*

Beep

Dietrich (*into the phone*) Nikki, this is Dietrich. Thank you, yes, I've got your message. I like also this message, by the way! So, I will take the train — that was my original idea, you know, before you kindly said you would meet me — and I will meet you at Victoria. Most unnecessary, but most nice of you ... Oh, Nikki, I'm so sorry to cause you all this trouble. So sorry about poor Chris going to Heathrow. Maybe my English was not quite clear ... But now this time — no mistake ... Victoria, yes? Not Waterloo, not King's Cross — Victoria! Anyway, thank you for a new experience — it was quite interesting for me to see the North Terminal ... Oh, what am I thinking of? You won't get this message — you're already on your way to Victoria!

The Lights cross-fade from Dietrich to Chris, at phone C. *He listens, rigid with irritation*

Dietrich moves to phone G

Nikki's Voice *Dietrich, so sorry, my idiot husband has gone to Heathrow, I told him Gatwick, and he went to Heathrow ...! Don't you listen to a single word I say? Not Dietrich — you! Dietrich, get on the train, there's a train, it goes to Victoria, come to Victoria, I'll jump in the car and meet you at Victoria. Victoria Station. So sorry — we're both longing to ——*

Beep

Chris (*into the phone*) Thank you for your charming message. If I sometimes
don't hear what you say at breakfast then it's because you say it while I'm
reading the newspaper, something I've warned you about a million times,
but I won't labour it again now, firstly because this morning I *did* hear you
— you said "Don't go to Gatwick". Or "Don't go to Heathrow". Or
something equally misleading. Secondly because this is my last coin, and
the phone's going to run out at any moment, and thirdly because you're not
there to hear it, since you're driving to Victoria to meet your chum, or
rather, *not* driving to Victoria, but walking hopelessly up and down the
street outside the house looking for the car, then slowly remembering that
the car's at Heathrow with me. And there's a fourth, rather more
important reason why I can't hang around here phoning you from
Terminal One at Heathrow, delightful as it is — because you seem to
have forgotten that ——

*We hear the dialling tone. He takes the receiver away from his ear and gazes
at it*

The Lights cross-fade from Chris to phone A

Nikki enters C, *rushes to the answering machine (phone A) and punches
"Record"*

Nikki (*into the answering machine*) No! CAN'T meet you at Victoria! No
car — car at Heathrow with idiot husband! DON'T WAIT, GET A TAXI
...! Hold on — no — you won't get this message — you're on the train —
I'll have to come on the Tube — only now I'm going to be late ... WAIT
AT VICTORIA ...! Oh, and Chris, in the future, if you've stopped listening
to anything I'm saying, will you at least have the courtesy to go ——

Beep

Exactly.

Nikki punches "Record", and runs out C

During the following, Nikki enters and moves to phone F

The Lights cross-fade from phone A to Chris, at phone C

Nikki's Voice ...*WAIT AT VICTORIA* ...! *Oh, and Chris, in the future, if
you've stopped listening to anything I'm saying, will you at least have the
courtesy to go* ——

Beep

Chris (*into the phone, calmly*) Yes, as I was saying, before the money ran out, and I had to go to the shop and buy myself a telephone card, because they wouldn't give me any change for the phone unless I bought something, so I bought a phone card for one pound, and I'd only got a twenty-pound note, and they only had small change, so now I've got a phone-card *and* nineteen pounds in loose change, which means that I can now stand here, with my trousers sagging a little under the weight of the coins, and talk to our answering machine for the rest of the night, except that I can't, because you've obviously forgotten, in all your excitement about meeting your lovely chum, about your mother arriving — something *I* reminded *you* about at breakfast, only you obviously weren't listening, even though you weren't reading the paper, even though I'd carefully got your attention before I began to speak — so I've got to come screaming back up the motorway to let her in, though by the time I get there, even as it is, she's likely to have been standing outside in the rain for some considerable time. Though of course if you've got this message you'll have got back and found her there yourself ...

The Lights cross-fade from Chris to Mother, at a coin-box in a public house (phone E), receiver to ear. She listens, puzzled, hand over her other ear. She has an umbrella with her

Chris moves to phone A

Nikki's Voice *...No! CAN'T meet you at Victoria! No car — car at Heathrow with idiot husband! DON'T WAIT, GET A TAXI ...! Hold on — no — you won't get this message — you're on the train — I'll have to come on the Tube — only now I'm going to be late ... WAIT AT VICTORIA ...! Oh, and Chris, in the future, if you've stopped listening to anything I'm saying, will you at least have the courtesy to go ...*

Beep

Mother (*into the phone*) Nicola, darling, it's Mummy. Oh dear, I hope everything's all right ... I can't quite understand what you're saying about Victoria — the noise here is simply frightful. I'm not at Victoria, darling — why do you think I'm at Victoria? I'm in a public house called the *Bag O'Nails*, just round the corner from you — I couldn't find a phone anywhere else ... I can't think for the noise ... Can you hear what I'm saying ...? I rang your bell ... I'm not quite sure what's happening ... I looked through the letter-box, and I thought I could hear Christopher's voice ...

Perhaps you're having some sort of ... little talk about things together. If so I'll wait here, of course ... There are some quite strange people in here ... Care in the community, I suppose. Nicola, darling, I do find it odd that you should want to live in a neighbourhood like this ... though of course it's nothing to do with me. I'll try to wait here until ... well, until.

The Lights cross-fade from Mother to Nikki, at a coin-box in an Underground station (phone F), receiver to ear. She listens impatiently

Mother moves to phone H

Nikki's Voice   ... *WAIT AT VICTORIA ...! Oh, and Chris, in the future, if you've stopped listening to anything I'm saying, will you at least have the courtesy to go* ——

Beep

Nikki (*into the phone*) Oh God, I thought you'd be back by now ... I'm at the Tube — I was on my way to Victoria to meet Dietrich — only I suddenly remembered Mummy's arriving ... You'll have to let her in ... Only you're not there, of course ... Oh no! She must be on the doorstep ...! I'll have to come back — *you'll* have to go to Victoria. He's going to be waiting at Victoria ... He's not *my* friend. I don't know why you say he's *my* friend. You hate it when I call people *your* friends instead of *our* friends ... Wait for Mummy first, if she's not there, then go to Victoria ... No, don't wait for Mummy, I'll deal with Mummy, don't do anything complicated — just GO TO VICTORIA!

The Lights cross-fade from Nikki to Chris at the answering machine (phone A)

Nikki's Voice   ... *No, don't wait for Mummy, I'll deal with Mummy, don't do anything complicated — just GO TO VICTORIA!*

There is a long beep

Chris presses "Record"

Chris (*into the answering machine*) No, your mother's not on the doorstep. I've just got back and found a message from her saying she's in a particularly sordid and notorious local pub. So I will go and fetch her out of it before she's murdered by drug-dealers. Nikki, you go to Victoria. Mother and Dietrich — you both stay EXACTLY WHERE YOU ARE!

Beep

Chris presses "Record"

The Lights cross-fade from Chris to Dietrich at a call-box in a railway station (phone G)

Chris moves to phone E

Chris's Voice ... *Nikki, you go to Victoria. Mother and Dietrich — you both stay EXACTLY WHERE YOU ARE!*
Dietrich (*into the phone*) Well, here I am at Victoria. And yes, of course, thank you, I wait here, exactly where I am ... Only that sounds bad about Nikki's mother and the drug-dealers ... I'm so sorry ... I'm afraid I'm causing you a big disruption. Well, I wait here ——

The Lights cross-fade from Dietrich to Chris at phone E

  Dietrich exits

Chris's Voice   — *both stay EXACTLY WHERE YOU ARE!*

Beep

Chris (*into the phone*) Right, I'm at the pub. Only of course your mother isn't here. I asked someone at the bar if they'd seen anyone who looked like your mother, and he offered me a snort of cocaine ... Now what ...? Perhaps just give up ... Give up on everything, toot the coke ...

The Lights cross-fade from Chris to Nikki at the answering machine (phone A)

Chris moves to phone H

Chris's Voice ... *Perhaps just give up ... Give up on everything, toot the coke ...*

There is a long beep

Nikki punches "Record"

Beep

Nikki (*into the answering machine*) Chris, I'm back — stay at the pub ... Which pub, incidentally? Why don't you say which pub? Anyway, I'll search the streets, in case ... Dietrich — so sorry, you must think we're all going totally crazy ... (*She punches "Record"*)

Beep

The Lights cross-fade from Nikki to Mother at a coin-box in a fast-food outlet (phone H)

Nikki exits

Nikki's Voice ... *Anyway, I'll search the streets, in case ... Dietrich — so sorry, you must think we're all going totally crazy ...*

Beep

Mother (*into the phone*) Nicola, darling, it's Mummy again. Oh, dear, I'm very sorry — I'm in a kind of restaurant in the High Street. It's called Spud-U-Like. I didn't want you coming into that terrible public house ... But Chris is there, is he? I'd better go back there. Don't worry. I'll be all right in there — I've got my umbrella.

The Lights cross-fade from Mother to the answering machine (phone A)

Nikki's Voice ... *Anyway, I'll search the streets, in case ... Dietrich — so sorry, you must think we're all going totally crazy ...*

Beep

The Lights cross-fade from the answering machine to Chris, at phone H

Chris (*into the phone*) Oh, so now you're out wandering the streets? I told you to stay where you were! Why don't you EVER LISTEN TO WHAT I SAY ...? I've now wasted the entire evening struggling to locate your friends and relations ... I've looked in every single café and bar along the High Street. I'm now in Spud-U-Like ... I'll try the house again ...

The Lights cross-fade from Chris to the answering machine

Chris exits

Nikki's Voice ... *Anyway, I'll search the streets, in case ... Dietrich — so sorry, you must think we're all going totally crazy ...*

Beep

   Nikki enters and moves to phone H

The Lights cross-fade from the answering machine to phone H

Nikki (*into the phone*) I suppose you're still in the pub ... Wherever it is ...
   I've looked in all the cafés and bars along the High Street ... I'm in Spud-
   U-Like ... I'll go back to the house ...

The Lights go down on Nikki

Nikki moves to phone I

   Dietrich enters and moves to phone E

The Lights come up on Dietrich at phone E, suitcase at his feet, hand to ear

Nikki's Voice ... *Dietrich — so sorry, you must think we're all going totally*
   crazy ...

Beep

Dietrich (*into the phone*) It's Dietrich again, I'm afraid. Can you hear this?
   I am calling from a rather noisy place. So, well, I waited at Victoria for some
   time, not very long, an hour perhaps, but clearly I have not understood quite
   right, so I took a taxi, and I came to your house ... I thought I hear voices
   inside, but no-one answers the bell ... It's raining, so I am waiting in a pub
   called the *Bag O'Nails*, which is an amusing name, but I think I must go
   soon, there is a somewhat bad atmosphere here ...

The Lights cross-fade from Dietrich to Nikki at a coin-box in the street (phone
I)

Dietrich moves to phone J

Nikki's Voice ... *Dietrich — so sorry, you must think we're all going totally*
   crazy ...

Beep

Nikki She's not at the house ... I'm so worried ... I'm at the phones in front
   of the police station ... They haven't had any reports of her ... I'll try all the
   pubs again ...

The Lights cross-fade from Nikki to the answering machine (phone A)

Nikki's Voice ... *Dietrich — so sorry, you must think we're all going totally crazy ...*

   Chris enters and moves to phone I

The Lights cross-fade from the answering machine to Chris at phone I

All the following dialogue is into the various phones

Beep

Chris You're *still* not back! Nikki, what the hell are you playing at ...? Listen, I'm at the phones in front of the police station — I'm going to report your mother missing ...

The Lights cross-fade from Chris to Dietrich at a coin-box in a hospital (phone J), bandaged, minus suitcase

Chris moves to phone E

Nikki's Voice ... *we're all going totally crazy ...*

Beep

Dietrich Hallo, it's Dietrich ... Dietrich ... I can't talk very clear ... There is a problem with my jaw ... My jaw ... Not to worry, everyone is very kind, I am at the Royal Infirmary. All my fault, I'm afraid. They say I should have rolled up like a ball and covered my head. But I have to ask another favour, because I regret to say I lost sight of my suitcase while I was unconscious ... Or maybe I can buy a toothbrush here ... (*He puts his hand in his pocket*) Wait — I call you back ... (*He hangs up and remains at the phone, feeling all his pockets*)

The Lights come up on Mother at a coin-box inside a police-station (phone K)

Nikki's Voice ... *we're all going totally crazy ...*

Beep

Mother Nicola, darling, I'm at the police station. Now, don't worry, darling, they arrested me in that public house, it's quite ludicrous — how you can live in a neighbourhood like this ... Anyway, they're charging me with assault, and it's all very ridiculous — I was simply trying to stop these people kicking this nice German gentleman, but if you could possibly come here and arrange bail ... I think I'll try to hold on until you come in, because they only let you make one call ... (*She remains at the phone*)

The Lights come up on Chris at phone E, receiver in one ear, hand to other

Chris (*into the phone; shouting*) Is that you?
Call Waiting (*voice-over*) *Please hold the line while we try to connect you.*
Chris Listen, I'm back in the Bag O'Nails ...
Call Waiting (*voice-over*) *The number you are calling knows you are waiting.*
Chris I can't hear a word you're saying — it's getting more hellish in here by the moment ...

The Lights come up on Nikki at a second call-box in the public house (phone L), just behind Chris's back. She dials furiously, elbowing Chris

Call Waiting (*voice-over*) *Please hold the line while we try to connect you.*
Chris (*shouting*) What?
Call Waiting (*voice-over*) *The number you are calling knows you are waiting.*
Chris You'll have to shout ...
Call Waiting (*voice-over*) *Please try later. The person you are calling is engaged on another call.*
Chris (*understanding*) Oh, no! (*He slams the receiver down and stands roaring with frustration*)

Dietrich, at phone J, dials

Nikki (*shouting*) Listen, I'm in a dreadful pub called the *Bag O'Nails* ...
Chris (*screaming*) I'm going to spend the rest of my life talking to electronic ghosts!
Nikki What? There's some drunken lunatic shouting in my ear ...
Call Waiting (*voice-over*) *The number you are calling knows you are waiting.*
Nikki *Who's* waiting?
Call Waiting (*voice-over*) *Please hold the line while we try to connect you.*
Nikki Try to what?
Call Waiting (*voice-over*) *The number you are calling knows you are waiting.*

Nikki Who am I talking to?
Call Waiting (*voice-over*) *Please try later. The person you are calling is engaged on another call.*

Nikki screams. She and Chris frantically re-dial

Mother Hallo? I'm not sure how much longer they'll let me hold on ...
Call Waiting (*voice-over*) *Please hold the line while we try to connect you.*
Dietrich Hallo, Nikki, yes, thank you, I hold the line ...
Call Waiting (*voice-over*) *The number you are calling knows you are waiting.*
Dietrich Waiting, yes, at the hospital, because now sadly also my wallet has gone astray ...
Mother Or you could pop some overnight things in a bag for me and I could stay in prison, if that would be more convenient.
Chris (*furiously*) Hallo?
Nikki (*furiously*) Hallo?
Mother (*anxiously*) Hallo?
Dietrich (*patiently*) Hallo?

Now everyone speaks or shouts at once

Chris Will you put the phone down, you stupid woman, and listen to what I'm saying? You've been yattering away for the past hour ...
Nikki Will you shut up, whoever you are, and put the phone down, and listen to what I'm saying, before I go completely out of my mind ...?
Mother Will you be sure to include some disinfectant, and some sort of insect-powder, in case conditions in the cell are not all they might be ...?
Dietrich And I think my passport, yes, and my watch, though fortunately it was not a valuable one, only two or three hundred marks ...
Call Waiting (*as blandly as ever, but raising its voice to shout them down*) *Please don't waste your breath. The machine you are calling is taking refuge in a breakdown.*

The answering machine explodes

CURTAIN

FURNITURE AND PROPERTY LIST

ACT I

ALARMS

On stage: Dining table. *On it*: bottle of wine, ingenious corkscrew
                   Four chairs
                   Side table. *On it*: telephone, answering machine

Off stage: Drawer containing several instruction books (**Jocasta**)
                   Large cast-iron saucepan (**John**)
                   Doorkeys (**John**)
                   Cordless phone (**Jocasta**)

DOUBLES

On stage: Two sets of:
                   Double bed
                   Bedside tables with practical lamps on them
                   TV with remote control
                   Fitted wall unit including luggage stand, hanging space, built-in desk
                       with practical lamp. *On desk*: hotel services directory
                   Mini-bar with biscuits
                   Electric kettle
                   Trouser-press

Off stage: Overnight bag, other travel impedimenta (**Miles**)
                   Bags and coats (**Melanie**)
                   Overnight bag, other travel impedimenta (**Laurence**)
                   Bags — including handbag with make-up — and coats (**Lynn**)
                   Toothbrush (**Laurence**)
                   Towels (**Laurence**)

ACT II

LEAVINGS

The same set and furniture as ALARMS

On stage: Dining table. *On it*: four empty wine glasses, bottle of wine
                   Four chairs
                   Side table. *On it*: telephone, answering machine

LOOK AWAY NOW

On stage: Three aircraft seats
                Newspapers for **Aptly**, **Bloss** and **Charr**

HEART TO HEART

No props

GLASSNOST

On stage: Lectern with microphones
                Glass Autocue plates

TOASTERS

On stage: Table. *On it*: nearly-empty wine bottle
                Three sets of: plate, knife and fork, napkin, wine glass, folder of papers
                  (**Spott**, **Much** and **Candle**)

IMMOBILES

On stage: Twelve telephones:
                Phone A: domestic phone with an answering machine, c
                Phone B: coin-box in an airport location, L
                Phone C: another coin-box in another airport location, R
                Phone D: yet another airport location
                Phone E: coin-box in a public house (with phone L right next to it)
                Phone F: coin-box at an Underground station.
                Phone G: call-box in a railway station
                Phone H: coin-box in a fast-food outlet
                Phone I: coin-box in the street
                Phone J: coin-box in a hospital
                Phone K: coin-box inside a police station

                Suitcase for **Dietrich**

Personal: **Mother**: umbrella

LIGHTING PLOT

ACT I

ALARMS

Practical fittings required: nil
Interior

To open: General interior lighting

Cue 1   **John** exits   (Page 22)
               Cut light spill from kitchen

DOUBLES

Practical fittings required: four bedside lamps
Composite set: two bedrooms with boxed-off shower/toilet units

To open: Darkness

Cue 2   **Miles** enters lefthand room   (Page 24)
               Bring up main lights on lefthand room

Cue 3   **Melanie** exits into the lefthand bathroom   (Page 25)
               Snap on lights in lefthand bathroom

Cue 4   **Miles**: " ... be staying in tomorrow night?"   (Page 25)
               Cut lights in lefthand bathroom

Cue 5   **Melanie** exits into lefthand bathroom   (Page 27)
               Snap on lights in lefthand bathroom

Cue 6   **Laurence** enters righthand room   (Page 28)
               Bring up main lights on righthand room

Cue 7   **Lynn** exits into the righthand bathroom   (Page 29)
               Snap on lights in righthand bathroom

Cue 8   **Laurence**: "More biscuits ..."   (Page 29)
               Cut lights in righthand bathroom

Cue 9   **Laurence** exits into the righthand bathroom   (Page 31)
               Snap on lights in righthand bathroom

| *Cue* 10 | **Miles** and **Lynn** turn on the TVs | (Page 32) |
| | *Bring up TV flicker from both televisions* | |

| *Cue* 11 | The news is replaced by a love scene | (Page 32) |
| | *Snap off both bathroom lights* | |

| *Cue* 12 | **Melanie** and **Laurence** switch the TVs off | (Page 33) |
| | *Cut TV flicker* | |

| *Cue* 13 | **Miles** and **Lynn** switch off the main room lights | (Page 39) |
| | *Cut main room lights in both rooms* | |

| *Cue* 14 | **Miles** enters the lefthand room | (Page 39) |
| | *Bring up lights on lefthand room* | |

| *Cue* 15 | **Miles** switches off the lights in the lefthand room | (Page 40) |
| | *Cut lights in lefthand room* | |

| *Cue* 16 | All four appear in the doorways | (Page 40) |
| | *Bring up bedside lights in both rooms* | |

| *Cue* 17 | **Melanie** and **Laurence** switch on the main lights | (Page 40) |
| | *Bring up main lights in both rooms* | |

| *Cue* 18 | **Melanie** exits into the lefthand bathroom | (Page 41) |
| | *Snap on light in lefthand bathroom* | |

| *Cue* 19 | **Lynn** exits into the righthand bathroom | (Page 41) |
| | *Snap on light in righthand bathroom* | |

| *Cue* 20 | **Miles**: " ... avoiding each other's eye." | (Page 43) |
| | *Snap off light in lefthand bathroom* | |

| *Cue* 21 | **Miles**: " ... I'll clean my teeth ever so quick!" | (Page 43) |
| | *Snap off light in righthand bathroom* | |

| *Cue* 22 | **Miles** goes into the lefthand bathroom | (Page 44) |
| | *Snap on light in lefthand bathroom* | |

| *Cue* 23 | **Laurence** exits into the righthand bathroom | (Page 44) |
| | *Snap on light in righthand bathroom* | |

| *Cue* 24 | **Laurence**: "'That's funny, he didn't say 'Good-evening'.'" | (Page 46) |
| | *Snap off light in lefthand bathroom* | |

| *Cue* 25 | **Laurence** exits into the righthand bathroom | (Page 47) |
| | *Snap off light in righthand bathroom* | |

Cue 26   **Miles** and **Laurence** turn out the side lights and main lights (Page 48)
            Cut all lights (in sequence with actors)

Cue 27   When ready   (Page 48)
            *Bring up **Miles**'s side light*

Cue 28   **Miles** switches his side light off   (Page 48)
            *Cut **Miles**'s side light*

Cue 29   **Melanie**: "I've said — yes!"   (Page 49)
            *Bring up **Miles**'s side light*

Cue 30   **Melanie** turns out the light   (Page 50)
            *Cut **Miles**'s side light*

Cue 31   **Lynn**: "I love you, too." Pause   (Page 50)
            *Bring up **Lynn**'s side light*

Cue 32   **Lynn** switches her light out   (Page 50)
            *Cut **Lynn**'s side light*

Cue 33   **Lynn**: "I'm waiting."   (Page 50)
            *Bring up **Miles**'s side light*

Cue 34   **Miles**. " ... Kevin and Sharon jealous."   (Page 51)
            *Bring up **Lynn**'s side light*

Cue 35   **Miles** and Laurence switch their lights out   (Page 53)
            *Cut **Miles**'s and **Laurence**'s side lights*

Cue 36   **Miles** gives a cry of pain   (Page 53)
            Bring up TV flicker in lefthand room

Cue 37   **Melanie**: "Oh, my God!"   (Page 54)
            *Bring up **Melanie**'s and **Laurence**'s side lights*

Cue 38   **Melanie** presses the fourth button   (Page 55)
            Cut TV flicker

Cue 39   **Laurence** turns off the side light   (Page 57)
            *Cut **Laurence**'s side light*

Cue 40   **Miles** exits into the lefthand bathroom   (Page 57)
            Bring up light in lefthand bathroom

Cue 41   **Lynn** turns on her side light   (Page 58)
            *Bring up **Lynn**'s side light*

Cue 42   **Laurence** turns the light out   (Page 58)
              Cut **Lynn**'s *side light*

Cue 43   **Lynn** turns on her side light   (Page 58)
              Bring up **Lynn**'s *side light*

Cue 44   **Laurence** turns the light out   (Page 58)
              Cut **Lynn**'s *side light*

Cue 45   **Lynn** turns on her side light   (Page 58)
              Bring up **Lynn**'s *side light*

Cue 46   **Laurence** turns the light out   (Page 58)
              Cut **Lynn**'s *side light*

Cue 47   **Lynn**'s light goes out   (Page 58)
              Cut lights in lefthand bathroom

Cue 48   **Lynn** turns on her side light   (Page 59)
              Bring up **Lynn**'s *side light*

Cue 49   **Melanie** and **Lynn** turn out their lights (Page 59)
              Cut **Melanie**'s *and* **Lynn**'s *lights*

Cue 50   Phrase of music   (Page 59)
              Grey light; pink light; dawn

Cue 51   **Laurence** exits into righthand bathroom   (Page 60)
              Snap on lights in righthand bathroom

Cue 52   **Miles** exits into lefthand bathroom   (Page 60)
              Snap on lights in lefthand bathroom

Cue 53   **Lynn**: "Never wants to *meet* anyone!"   (Page 62)
              Snap off both bathroom lights

Cue 54   **Lynn** exits into the righthand bathroom   (Page 65)
              Snap on lights in righthand bathroom

Cue 55   **Miles**: " ... going to get on like a house on fire." (Page 66)
              Snap off lights in righthand bathroom

ACT II

LEAVINGS

Practical fittings required: nil
Interior

To open: General interior lighting

No cues

LOOK AWAY NOW

Practical fittings required: nil
Aircraft interior

To open: General interior lighting

No cues

HEART TO HEART

Practical fittings required: nil
Interior

To open: General interior lighting

No cues

GLASSNOST

Practical fittings required: nil
Interior

To open: Darkness

Cue 56   **Voice over PA** "My Lords, Ladies and Gentlemen ... "   (Page 89)
                Lights up on lectern and microphones

TOASTERS

Practical fittings required: nil
Interior

To open: General interior lighting

No cues

IMMOBILES

Practical fittings required: nil
Twelve telephones

To open: Darkness

Cue 57   Phone rings; when ready   (Page 99)
               Bring up lights on phone A

Cue 58   Beep   (Page 99)
               Bring up lights on phone B; fade lights on phone A

Cue 59   **Dietrich**: " ... your humorous message, by the way."   (Page 99)
               Cross-fade lights from phone B to phone C

Cue 60   **Chris**: "*Two*, yes?"   (Page 100)
               Cross-fade lights from phone C to phone B

Cue 61   **Dietrich**: "I look forward to see you."   (Page 100)
               Cross-fade lights from phone B to phone A

Cue 62   **Nikki** presses "Record"   (Page 101)
               Cross-fade lights from phone A to phone B

Cue 63   **Dietrich**: "Sorry to be such a pain in the behind."   (Page 101)
               Cross-fade lights from phone B to phone C

Cue 64   **Chris**: " — he's your chum, not mine."   (Page 101)
               Cross-fade lights from phone C to phone B

Cue 65   **Dietrich**: " ... to take all this trouble ..."   (Page 102)
               Cross-fade lights from phone B to phone D

Cue 66   **Chris**: " — *don't* go somewhere."   (Page 102)
               Cross-fade lights from phone D to phone A

Cue 67   **Nikki** punches "Record"   (Page 103)
               Cross-fade lights from phone A to phone B

Cue 68   **Dietrich**: " ... on your way to Victoria!"   (Page 103)
               Cross-fade lights from phone B to phone C

Cue 69   **Chris** gazes at the receiver   (Page 104)
               Cross-fade lights from phone C to phone A

Cue 70   **Nikki** runs out c   (Page 104)
               Cross-fade lights from phone A to phone C

Cue 71	**Chris**: " ... found her there yourself ... " *Cross-fade lights from phone C to phone E*	(Page 105)
Cue 72	**Mother**: " ... well, until." *Cross-fade lights from phone E to phone F*	(Page 106)
Cue 73	**Nikki**: " — just GO TO VICTORIA!" *Cross-fade lights from phone F to phone A*	(Page 106)
Cue 74	**Chris** presses "Record" *Cross-fade lights from phone A to phone G*	(Page 107)
Cue 75	**Dietrich**: "Well, I wait here ——" *Cross-fade lights from phone G to phone E*	(Page 107)
Cue 76	**Chris**: " ... toot the coke ..." Cross-fade lights from phone E to phone A	(Page 107)
Cue 77	**Nikki** punches "Record". Beep *Cross-fade lights from phone A to phone H*	(Page 108)
Cue 78	**Mother**: " — I've got my umbrella." *Cross-fade lights from phone H to phone A*	(Page 108)
Cue 79	**Nikki's Voice**: " ... *totally crazy* ..." *Cross-fade lights from phone A to phone H*	(Page 108)
Cue 80	**Chris**: "I'll try the house again ..." *Cross-fade lights from phone H to phone A*	(Page 108)
Cue 81	Beep. **Nikki** moves to phone H *Cross-fade lights from phone A to phone H*	(Page 109)
Cue 82	**Nikki**: "I'll go back to the house ..." *Fade lights on* **Nikki**	(Page 109)
Cue 83	*Dietrich moves to phone E* *Bring up lights on phone E*	(Page 109)
Cue 84	**Dietrich**: " ... bad atmosphere here ..." *Cross-fade lights from phone E to phone I*	(Page 109)
Cue 85	**Nikki**: "I'll try all the pubs again ..." *Cross-fade lights from phone I to phone A*	(Page 109)
Cue 86	**Nikki's Voice**: " ... *totally crazy* ..." Cross-fade lights from phone A to phone I	(Page 110)

Cue 87   **Chris**: " ... report your mother missing ... "   (Page 110)
              Cross-fade lights from phone I to phone J

Cue 88   **Dietrich** remains at the phone, feeling his pockets   (Page 110)
              Bring up lights on phone K

Cue 89   **Mother**: " ... they only let you make one call ... "   (Page 111)
              Bring up lights on phone E

Cue 90   **Chris**: " ... more hellish in here by the moment ..."   (Page 111)
              Bring up lights on phone L

EFFECTS PLOT

ACT I

ALARMS

Cue 14	**Jocasta**: "The oven doesn't go ——" *Chink*	(Page 5)
Cue 15	**Jocasta**: "The timer thing goes ——" *Continuous buzz*	(Page 5)
Cue 16	**Nicholas**: "The coffee-grinder." *Cut buzzing*	(Page 6)
Cue 17	**John**: "How can a toaster go ——?" *Chink*	(Page 6)
Cue 18	**John**: "I'm trying to." *Continuous buzz*	(Page 6)
Cue 19	**Jocasta**: "I'm trying to!" *Cut buzzing*	(Page 7)
Cue 20	**Nicholas**: "At least we haven't got the ——" *Chink*	(Page 7)
Cue 21	**Nancy**: "Now it's trapped somewhere." *Chink*	(Page 7)
Cue 22	**Nancy**: "It's getting desperate." *Chink*	(Page 7)
Cue 23	**Nancy**: "It's in the ceiling." They watch *Chink*	(Page 7)
Cue 24	They all sniff *Continuous buzz*	(Page 8)
Cue 25	**Jocasta** exits R *Cut buzzing. Chink*	(Page 8)
Cue 26	**John** puts the book back in the pile *Chink*	(Page 8)
Cue 27	**Nicholas**: "Things don't go ——" *Chink*	(Page 9)
Cue 28	**Nicholas**: " ... at least it won't keep going ——" *Chink. Continuous buzz*	(Page 9)
Cue 29	**Jocasta** exits R *Phone rings*	(Page 9)

| *Cue* 30 | **Nicholas** answers the phone | (Page 9) |
| | *Cut phone ring* | |

| *Cue* 31 | **Nicholas**: "Rather urgent." | (Page 9) |
| | *Cut buzz* | |

| *Cue* 32 | **Jocasta**: " ... remember what to press!" | (Page 10) |
| | *Continuous buzz* | |

| *Cue* 33 | **John**: "What is it?" | (Page 10) |
| | *Chink* | |

| *Cue* 34 | **John**: "I can't think with that buzzer going!" | (Page 11) |
| | *Chink* | |

| *Cue* 35 | **John**: "We'll hear it on the answering machine ... " | (Page 11) |
| | *Chink* | |

| *Cue* 36 | **Nicholas**: "You open the wine." | (Page 12) |
| | *Chink* | |

| *Cue* 37 | **Nicholas** exits C | (Page 12) |
| | *Car alarm* | |

| *Cue* 38 | **Nancy** acts to work with the corkscrew | (Page 12) |
| | *Cut buzzer* | |

| *Cue* 39 | **Jocasta** exits R | (Page 12) |
| | *Doorbell* | |

| *Cue* 40 | **Jocasta** exits R | (Page 13) |
| | **Answering Machine Voice**, *dialogue as p. 13 (5 lines)* | |

| *Cue* 41 | **Jocasta**: "Study! Study!" | (Page 13) |
| | *Doorbell* | |

| *Cue* 42 | **Jocasta**: "*I'll* go!" | (Page 14) |
| | *Continuous buzz* | |

| *Cue* 43 | **John**: "Nothing happens!" | (Page 14) |
| | **Answering Machine Voice**, *dialogue as p. 14* | |

| *Cue* 44 | **John**: "Oh, good." | (Page 14) |
| | **Answering Machine Voice**, *dialogue as p. 14* | |

| *Cue* 45 | **John**: "I have not the faintest notion!" | (Page 14) |
| | *Car alarm* | |

Cue 46   **John** and **Nicholas** exit L   (Page 15)
             Answering Machine Voice, *dialogue as p. 15*

Cue 47   **Jocasta**: "*I'll* tell him."   (Page 16)
             Cut car alarm

Cue 48   **John**: "Where is everybody?"   (Page 17)
             Answering Machine Voice, *dialogue as p. 17*

Cue 49   **Nancy** puts her head between her knees   (Page 18)
             Cut buzz

Cue 50   **Jocasta** exits L   (Page 20)
             Answering Machine *voice, dialogue as p. 20*

Cue 51   **John** sets the alarm   (Page 20)
             Four pips from burglar alarm followed by warbling tone

Cue 52   **Jocasta** bundles **John** and **Nicholas** off L   (Page 20)
             Front door slams; continuous tone from the burglar alarm;
                Answering Machine Voice, *dialogue as p. 20*

Cue 53   **John**: "I've got the keys!"   (Page 21)
             Front door opens; continuous tone from burglar alarm
                turns to urgent interrupted warning tone

Cue 54   **Jocasta** operates the alarm   (Page 21)
             Four pips from burglar alarm

Cue 55   **Jocasta** operates the alarm   (Page 21)
             Four pips, followed by a warbling tone

Cue 56   **John** exits R   (Page 22)
             Slam of front door, continuous tone from burglar alarm

Cue 57   **Jocasta**: "What are you playing at?"   (Page 22)
             Hammering on front door

Cue 58   **John**: "Four nothing ..."   (Page 22)
             Answering Machine Voice, *dialogue as p. 22 (4 lines)*

Cue 59   **John**: "I'll tell you *my* side of the story ..."   (Page 23)
             Burgar alarm, doorbell, car alarm, approaching police siren

DOUBLES

Cue 60	**Miles** and **Lynn** turn on the TVs *Sound of announcer reading news bulletin in* *"Rewindese" (the language a recording makes* *when it's run backwards)*	(Page 32)
Cue 61	**Miles** and **Lynn** press the remotes *Sound of Rewindese love scene*	(Page 32)
Cue 62	**Miles** and **Lynn** press the remotes again *Sound of Rewindese news*	(Page 32)
Cue 63	**Melanie** and **Laurence** press the remotes *Sound of Rewindese love scene*	(Page 32)
Cue 64	The lefthand room door closes *Music for a moment*	(Page 40)
Cue 65	**Laurence**: "... a hint of moles' armpits." *Lavatory flush from lefthand bathroom*	(Page 41)
Cue 66	**Miles**: "Laurence and *Lynn*?" *Lavatory flush from righthand bathroom*	(Page 42)
Cue 67	**Laurence** (*off*) " ... for your benefit!" *Lavatory flush from lefthand bathroom*	(Page 44)
Cue 68	**Laurence** goes back into the righthand bathroom *Lavatory flush from righthand bathroom*	(Page 46)
Cue 69	**Miles** and **Laurence** turn out the lights *Music for a moment*	(Page 53)
Cue 70	**Miles** gives a cry of pain *Gunfight, very loud, dramatic music and* *shouts in Rewindese from lefthand TV*	(Page 53)
Cue 71	**Melanie** *presses the remote* *Low-grade Rewindese porn, hugely loud*	(Page 55)
Cue 72	**Melanie** presses the remote again *Increase volume of TV sound*	(Page 55)
Cue 73	**Melanie** presses the remote again *Increase volume of TV sound*	(Page 55)
Cue 74	**Melanie** presses the remote again *Cut TV sound*	(Page 55)

Cue 75   **Melanie** and **Lynn** turn out their lights   (Page 59)
              Phrase of music

ACT II

LEAVINGS

Cue 76   **John** and **Jocasta** settle at the table   (Page 80)
              Chink

LOOK AWAY NOW

Cue 77   As play begins   (Page 81)
              Reassuring music

Cue 78   When ready
              Cut reassuring music; then , **Stewardess** *voice-over,*
                  dialogue as pp.82-84

HEART TO HEART

Cue 79   As play begins   (Page 85)
              Confused and deafening roar of party conversation

Cue 80   **Charmian**: "What?"   (Page 85)
              Fade party conversation roar during following

Cue 81   **Clifford** and **Peter** take hold of **Charmian**   (Page 88)
              Bring up party conversation roar to level of cue 79

Cue 82   The two men pull **Charmian** in different directions   (Page 88)
              Huge cosmic laughter

GLASSNOST

Cue 83   As play begins   (Page 89)
              Hubbub of audience

Cue 84   When ready   (Page 89)
              Voice over PA — dialogue as p. 89

Cue 85   **Voice over PA** "My Lords, Ladies and Gentlemen ..."   (Page 89)
              Hubbub dies away

Cue 86   **The Baroness** enters (Page 89)
              Tumultuous applause

TOASTERS

Cue 87   When ready   (Page 93)
            Speaker's Voice *over speakers — dialogue as pp. 93-98*

Cue 88   **Speaker's Voice:** " ... be congratulated ..."   (Page 94)
            Uncertain applause

Cue 89   **Speaker's Voice:** " ... a round of applause."   (Page 95)
            Applause

Cue 90   **Speaker's Voice:** " ... efficiency award ——"   (Page 95)
            Uncertain applause

Cue 91   They drink the toast   (Page 96)
            Applause

Cue 92   **Everyone:** "James Trodden!"   (Page 96)
            Applause

Cue 93   **Speaker's Voice:** " ... this anniversary possible ..."   (Page 94)
            Applause

Cue 94   **Speaker's Voice:** " ... up and down the country ..."   (Page 94)
            Applause

Cue 95   **Speaker's Voice:** " — and clapping *at the same time*."." (Page 94)
            Applause; huge sound of chinking and smashing glass

IMMOBILES

Cue 96   As play begins   (Page 99)
            Phone ringing

Cue 97   Lights come up on phone A   (Page 99)
            Answering machine, dialogue as p.99, then beep

Cue 98   Lights cross-fade to **Chris**   (Page 100)
            *Ringing tone: brr, brr, brr; then answering machine,
                dialogue as p. 100, then beep*

Cue 99   Lights cross-fade to **Dietrich**   (Page 100)
            *Ringing tone: brr, brr, brr; then answering machine,
                dialogue as p. 100, then beep*

Cue 100   Lights cross-fade to **Nikki**   (Page 100)
            Answering machine, dialogue as p. 100, then long beep

Cue 101	**Nikki**: " ... have to fit the outgoing message into ——" *Beep*	(Page 101)
Cue 102	Lights cross-fade to **Dietrich** *Answering machine, dialogue as p. 101, then beep*	(Page 101)
Cue 103	Lights cross-fade to **Chris** *Answering machine, dialogue as p. 101, then beep*	(Page 101)
Cue 104	Lights cross-fade to **Dietrich** *Answering machine, dialogue as p. 102, then beep*	(Page 102)
Cue 105	Lights cross-fade to **Chris** *Answering machine, dialogue as p. 102*	(Page 102)
Cue 106	Lights cross-fade to **Nikki** *Answering machine, dialogue as p. 102, then long beep*	(Page 102)
Cue 107	**Nikki**: " ... we're both longing to ——" *Beep*	(Page 103)
Cue 108	Lights cross-fade to **Dietrich** *Answering machine, dialogue as p. 103, then beep*	(Page 103)
Cue 109	Lights cross-fade to **Chris** *Answering machine, dialogue as p. 103, then beep*	(Page 103)
Cue 110	**Chris**: " ... you seem to have forgotten that ——" *Dialling tone*	(Page 104)
Cue 111	**Nikki**: " ... have the courtesy to go ——" *Beep*	(Page 104)
Cue 112	Lights cross-fade to **Chris** *Answering machine, dialogue as p. 104, then beep*	(Page 104)
Cue 113	Lights cross-fade to **Mother** *Answering machine, dialogue as p.105, then beep*	(Page 105)
Cue 114	Lights cross-fade to **Nikki** *Answering machine, dialogue as p. 106, then beep*	(Page 106)
Cue 115	Lights cross-fade to **Chris** *Answering machine, dialogue as p. 106, then long beep*	(Page 106)
Cue 116	**Chris**: " ... EXACTLY WHERE YOU ARE!" *Beep*	(Page 106)

Cue 117   Lights cross-fade to **Dietrich**   (Page 107)
            Answering machine, dialogue as p. 107

Cue 118   Lights cross-fade to **Chris**   (Page 107)
            Answering machine, dialogue as p. 107, then beep

Cue 119   Lights cross-fade to **Nikki**   (Page 107)
            Answering machine, dialogue as p. 107, then long beep

Cue 120   **Nikki** punches "Record"   (Page 107)
            Beep

Cue 121   **Nikki** punches "Record"   (Page 108)
            Beep

Cue 122   Lights cross-fade to **Mother**   (Page 108)
            Answering machine, dialogue as p. 108, then beep

Cue 123   Lights cross-fade to answering machine   (Page 108)
            Answering machine, dialogue as p. 108, then beep

Cue 124   Lights cross-fade to answering machine   (Page 108)
            Answering machine, dialogue as p. 108, then beep

Cue 125   Lights come up on **Dietrich**   (Page 109)
            Answering machine, dialogue as p. 109, then beep

Cue 126   Lights cross-fade to **Nikki**   (Page 109)
            Answering machine, dialogue as p. 109, then beep

Cue 127   Lights cross-fade to answering machine   (Page 110)
            Answering machine, dialogue as p. 110

Cue 128   Lights cross-fade to **Chris**   (Page 110)
            Beep

Cue 129   Lights cross-fade to **Dietrich**   (Page 110)
            Answering machine, dialogue as p. 110, then beep

Cue 130   Lights cross-fade to **Mother**   (Page 110)
            Answering machine, dialogue as p. 110, then beep

Cue 131   **Chris**: "Is that you?"   (Page 111)
            Call Waiting *voice-over; 12 lines pp. 111-112*

Cue 132   **Call Waiting**: " ... taking refuge in a breakdown."   (Page 112)
            Answering machine explodes